Rachel Smets

Living Abroad
Successfully

What Where When How

ISBN-13: 978-1975604974
ISBN-10: 1975604970

For any queries, contact me www.rachelsmets.com

*"You can have more than one home.
You can carry your roots with you,
and decide where they grow."*

– Henning Mankell

Table of Contents

Acknowledgments

I'm grateful to be able to share my experiences with you through this book.

To all the expats who have shared their personal journeys and stories, thank you for taking the time and effort to complete the interview and for passing on great tips and–most of all–for your inspiration.

To all my friends who encouraged me throughout and stand by my side, the ones who ask me how I'm doing and then take time to listen, thank you for your patience and support. Your belief and trust in me keeps me motivated. The patting on my back, telling me I'm doing just fine, is often all I need.

To everyone helping me make certain decisions along the way, thank you for providing your honest opinions.

To my dear brother, Reginald Smets, my greatest support in everything I do, thank you for always being there for me, no matter where, no matter what. When I feel the need to talk, you make time for me, and with one blink of an eye, you get me. Even if we don't see each other often, you boost my energy in an instant. You mean the world to me.

Last but not least, to my loving parents, Regine and Felix Smets, Thank you. Even if you don't always understand what or why I do things, you are always caring, proud and ready to help at any time. You have raised me to become independent and allowed me the liberty and freedom to move abroad and live my journey. I love you.

Without all of you, this book would never have been written. **Thank you.**

Your FREE GIFT!

As a way of saying **Thank You** for your purchase, I'd like to offer you these free **GIFTS**.

You can find your gifts here http://www.rachelsmets.com/living-abroad-successfully-free-gift/

GIFT #1: *Awaken Your Confidence Action Guide.* A practical, clear and effective guide to boost your confidence on a daily basis.

GIFT #2: *Top 5 Confidence Hacks.* A video taking your through the steps you can take to achieve your goals.

To receive your presents, just click here http://www.rachelsmets.com/living-abroad-successfully-free-gift/

If you want to make a change in your life, it's never too late.
Life changes and so can YOU!!!

Introduction

Imagine sitting on the terrace of a café, located in the heart of a city center. The sun is shining, the air is light and warm, the icy glass in your hand feels refreshing as you observe the passersby flowing and weaving through the streets. You feel a rush of excitement and pride when the waiter approaches to take your order and you're able to respond in some facsimile of fluency in the language of your new home. The atmosphere is charged with a sense of adventure and you can't help but daydream about your future in a new land. Taking a sip of your drink, you notice a small group of friends walk past, talking cheerfully and a twinge of loneliness stabs at your heart. Leaving everyone behind had been the hardest thing you've ever done, and for a moment, you doubt whether you made the right choice. Some things in life never change, no matter where you are in the world. As the friends move on, the beauty of the fountain across the square catches your eye and you're once more reminded of why you're there, why you've chosen the life of an expatriate.

The beauty, excitement, and charm of an expatriate experience, also reveals moments of doubt, uncertainty, and difficulty.

Before I decided to move abroad for the first time, it was because I couldn't get past the thought that I didn't want to grow old wondering, *if only I had done it*. Feelings of

11

guilt and regret are emotions I'd rather avoid and so, there was only one solution: take action!

Living and working abroad is a life-changing experience that *should* be astonishing and awe-inspiring. My intention is to prepare you for your big move by giving you the whole truth and nothing but the truth, —and leave you with a wonderful feeling that will last beyond your arrival in your new home.

The more you know about cultural differences, adjusting to life abroad, and typical situations expats often deal with, the better prepared you'll feel and the more positive your experience will be. This book will set the stage for you to direct the next chapter of your life.

A combination of experiences, expat interviews, quotes, and checklists are gathered in this book.

Topics that will be covered include:
- Planning and prioritizing
- Understanding your personal goals
- Maintaining relationships
- Managing finances, banking, and insurance, etc.
- Finding the right accommodations
- Occupation options
- Integrating into a new culture
- Settling in smoothly
- Learning the local language
- Getting to know the locals
- And much more...

I wrote this book to provide you with as much insight as possible about living your life abroad. I hope it helps you make decisions about whether your life's next great adventure will take place abroad and then help make the transition as smooth and easy as possible.

Whether you're single or married, with children or without, this book is for you. Maybe you're employed and being sent abroad by your organization, or maybe you've decided you need a change and want to move on your own. You can be a student, a volunteer, or someone dreaming of finding a job abroad. Each situation is different and some routes to living abroad may appear easier than others, but having experienced many of the above personally, I want to share my hours of research on the subject along with my firsthand knowledge with you.

Moving abroad is a journey full of opportunities and challenges that will strengthen you as a person, often unconsciously. You become more flexible, more adaptable to various situations, your intercultural knowledge will expand, and with every new interaction, you'll build new relationships. The amount of confidence you gain can be incredible and will provide you with extra benefits to all areas of life. You can read more about the subject in my bestseller, *AWAKEN YOUR CONFIDENCE: 15 People Share their Journey to Success*.

Any uncertainty or fear you're experiencing can be lessened, or avoided altogether, if you're well-prepared for what's to come.

Making the decision to move abroad isn't one to make lightly. You're taking a risk by leaving your familiar world to venture into the unknown. But no matter what your destination is, the journey will be a wealth of experiences nobody can take away from you. It's a time you'll be able to cherish for the rest of your life.

Before we dive in, I would like to explain how the term *expat* (abbreviation for expatriate) will be used in this book. Though a variety of definitions for this term exist, we'll hold onto the definition as being anyone who is living outside of his or her home country, on either a permanent or temporary basis.

What you will take away from this book depends on your current situation and goal. Because our lives and dreams change over time, you will be able to pick up this book again at a later date and find new inspiration and value in that moment.

The stories contained inside present the exhilaration, satisfaction, confusion, and frustration that are all part of being an expat. These quotations and confessions, I hope, will inspire you, sober you, make you laugh, and create new thoughts. This book is informative, as well as authentic via the true experiences and anecdotes. It's also a practical manual, including useful checklists you can use in your journey.

My expat life began in my early twenties, when I was married and working two jobs. In the salon I managed, most of my clients were expats. Talking to them, I became inspired by the idea of "life abroad." I wanted that experience for myself, traveling to a foreign country, learning about other cultures, other people, other places and different foods.

A new dream was born. Would it be a success, a failure, or a regret? Everything was possible, but one thing was sure: I would never have to wonder "what if I had done it?" I took action, without rushing, and small steps to plan and prepare myself as best I could without having a practical guide like this book.

Fast forward to today, I've moved about 12 times between seven different countries. That number is certainly not final and I haven't been back to my home country since. My adventurous journey is undoubtedly one to be continued.

Between all the people I've met out in the world, I don't know anyone who has regretted moving abroad, but I know plenty who have regretted staying behind.

So, read on and discover which road you will take! **Enjoy your journey**.

PART ONE

Chapter 1
The Psyche of an Expat

Imagine you are sitting in a crowded downtown coffee shop, observing the people around you. Off to one side, you notice a group of friends laughing hard while drinking beer, and on the other, you notice a mother with two young children, trying to clean up spilled orange juice with a napkin. Then you look down at your own hands holding a coffee cup. You are smiling and feeling relaxed and calm. You check in with yourself and pay attention to your own being.

So, who are you?

Your answer could be something like: I'm an engineer, or maybe a teacher. You might say, I'm unemployed, or I'm a student. And some of you may answer: I'm a son, a brother, a mother, or perhaps a loyal friend. Try looking even deeper inside, to the level of emotions, personality, longings, and needs. Are you generally calm and patient? Or nervous and anxious? Are you introverted or extroverted? Do you hate changes and love your daily routines? Maybe you enjoy your preferred coffee at your favourite café because they prepare it just as you want it. You meet your circle of friends every week to go out, catch up on the latest gossip, and have a good laugh. Or maybe you couldn't care less about where the party is because you do your own thing and enjoy yourself whether alone or with others.

Don't worry about answering all of these questions right away; the answers will become much clearer in this chapter.

Perhaps the *most* important factor is your attitude. Your own outlook will play a major role in determining your success or failure abroad. It helps greatly to be positive and open-minded. Since you already picked up this book, you've already shown you're interested and open to learning more, so you can tick off that box and consider yourself a step closer to broader possibilities in life.

Are you a globetrotter who travels as much as possible? Perhaps you're interested in travelling but never had the chance to do so. Or maybe you had a taste of living abroad as a student, and you want more. Volunteers or seasonal workers sometimes have a short experience abroad, which can make the decision to make an extended move much easier. Some expats will leave their home situation entirely, packing up everything, including furniture, and cancelling all utilities, insurances, etc. We'll talk about that more later on. Everybody is different and has their own reasons to stay or to go. In the end, only you can decide what is right for you.

Born and raised in Belgium, I grew up in a town called Overijse. As a child, I was very shy, silent, and not confident. My parents had to constantly push me to speak up when people talked to me. I simply had no self-esteem whatsoever. I felt I had nothing interesting to offer. I had no idea how wrong I was.

When I was about nine years old, my first true friend—my BFF—was American. Her family had moved overseas for her father's job. In other words, they were expats, but I'd never heard or used that term back then. All I wanted back then was to play together, keeping our verbal communication very simple. Yes. No. Here. There. Sometimes we'd just smile or point at something. It didn't seem like much at the time, but that was my introduction to the English language, which developed rapidly, along with my taste for new and different cultures.

Since then, my interest in other cultures and languages has never waned. Now, with nearly 7 languages and many countries under my belt, I've built amazing relationships all over the world. I'm still living abroad as I write this and am completely devoted to intercultural topics in a variety of different ways, from teaching to coaching and speaking. My curiosity is my drive to learn, and staying open-minded has brought me fascinating opportunities. I continue to enjoy this journey, day after day.

Did I always think this positively? In all honesty, in the past, I had my fair share of feeling miserable, sitting around, wondering, *why am I doing this? Why did I make the decision to move? I'm in a country where I know absolutely no one. Why is the paperwork so complicated? I just need an I.D. card so I can open an account and rent a place. Why does everything have to be so hard?*

One thing I taught myself early on is to shift my negative thoughts around. Maybe I learned that sooner because I lived alone and knew nobody would help me. So instead of letting myself stay down, I learned to pick myself up and move on. Whatever your situation, holding on to negative thoughts doesn't help. On the contrary, it keeps you in the vicious cycle of pessimism and depression. Constant worrying is no way to start your expat life! Generally, huge problems are rare and the majority of expats don't need to consider returning home ahead of plan.

Keep everything in context and try to stay in the present moment at all times. Don't focus on things that are temporarily going wrong, because most of the time, by taking small steps, day by day, everything will eventually fall into place.

If the idea of moving far away from home seems daunting, rest assured that you can learn to re-train your brain. It takes practice, but anybody can do it. But before you can retrain your thoughts, you must learn to be aware of them. The only way to do that is by observing yourself. Take a moment to watch yourself from a distance and then pay attention to your thoughts. Do you feel worry, fear, hopelessness, confidence, anger, or excitement? Once you're conscious of what goes on in your mind, you enter a level of awareness that makes it much easier to invite more positivity into your life. This doesn't happen overnight of course, and it definitely takes practice, every day. But there's no reason you can't start right now by paying close attention to yourself and your thoughts and feelings. You can go about it any way you want—even start journal if you'd like—but take a moment to reflect each and every day and you will find you benefit from it down the road.

If you like to know more about this process, you can find it as one of the confidence hacks explained in more detail in my book, *AWAKEN YOUR CONFIDENCE: 15 People Share their Journey to Success*.

> *"My biggest difficulty was the emotional side of moving. Although I was happy and together with my husband, I felt guilty for leaving my family behind. Especially after having children of my own, I felt bad because my mother couldn't see her granddaughters as often as she would if we were living closer. I learned to accept my decision, even if took a while, but now I live in peace and feel happy with the choice that we made."*
> **– Aline from Brazil.**

It's a great skill to be able to remain positive no matter how many challenges appear on your path. The SECRET is to turn challenges into opportunities and remember your experience abroad will ultimately be rewarding!

KEY TAKEAWAYS:

→ Observe yourself and find your true self
→ Notice your thoughts
→ Switch your negative into positive
→ Be open-minded

Chapter 2
Success is the Result of Preparation

"Research is what I'm doing when I don't know what I'm doing."
—Wernher von Braun

Let's say you want to a new kitchen in your house. You might begin by talking about it with friends and family, then start picking out images in magazines or online, or visit several stores to gather ideas and inspiration. Then you take the next step of measuring your available space, narrowing down your options for cupboards, counter-tops, and furniture. After weighing your options with regards to colour and design, you finally make a decision, order your new kitchen, and schedule the installation. Now you can start packing up the contents of your old kitchen to prepare for the new.

Preparation, research, and scheduling—these are the key ingredients in a cocktail called, *Abroad on the rocks*).

In case it's not yet clear, there's a lot more to moving abroad than simply hopping on a plane, singing, *everything will be alright*. Though I admire those spontaneous, unquestioning character traits, if you want the experience to be as smooth and enjoyable as possible, good preparation will go a long way toward achieving that

25

goal. Neglecting to do proper research may result in your dream of living abroad turning into a nightmare. Last-minute panic prior to departure or unpleasant surprises upon arrival are not uncommon. You don't want the next few years of your life to be a miserable mess, do you? Your tasty cocktail can turn into a bitter *digestif* very quickly.

Before running comes walking. Before moving abroad comes getting ready to move abroad. This can take months, a year, or longer. It's different for everyone. Depending on your situation, you might be going through administrative procedures, perhaps enrolling your children in school, organizing an international move, researching the cultural aspect of the expat adventure, taking language classes, or requesting information from experienced expats online about what types of things you should be doing to prepare. Don't panic! You don't have to know everything just yet! By the time you reach the end of this book, you'll have been through all the essential topics you need to consider.

Here's an overview of some of the preparatory topics that will be covered in detail in this book:
- **Researching your destination country**
  - Climate
  - Accommodations
  - Public transportation
  - Customs, religion, food
  - Utilities
- **Sort out your finances**
- **Getting a health check**
- **Vaccinations**

- **Insurance**
- **Schools** (if you have children)
- **Learning the language**
- **Passports and Visas**
- **Booking your tickets**
- **Canceling subscriptions, contracts, and residence registration**
- **Mail Forwarding and changing your address**
- **Documentation and Driver's license concerns**
- **Housing**
- **Banking**
- **Booking a moving company**
- **Selling items you may no longer need**
- **Bringing Pets along**
- **What to pack**

" We had 6 months prior to our move to prepare ourselves for such step. We had to go through loads of documents, certifications and hundreds of signatures. We did not really think what we might face, or whether it is bad or good, so we didn't prepare further than the requested papers. We wanted to move anyway, so as a family we were happy. And as we had NO preparation beforehand, this was one BIG challenge for us that we had no idea about. It is like jumping in the sea with no life jacket and we do not really know how to swim."

- Abdel from Egypt

Keep in mind that, although it is important to research your chosen destination carefully, you won't know what it's actually like to live there until you've made the move.

What is your next step? A question many people struggle with, in all areas of life. Whether shifting countries, careers, or even relationships, taking the next step is crucial for change to occur. You may find inspiration watching my TEDx talk about the subject. http://bit.ly/RachelSmets-TEDxTalk

KEY TAKEAWAYS:

→ Prepare, research, and plan
→ Use the checklists to make sure you've covered all the main topics
→ Ask other people about their experiences
→ Proper planning will make your move smooth and agreeable

Chapter 3
Money Matters

"A budget is telling your money where to go, instead of wondering where it went."
–John C. Maxwell

What a wonderful feeling it is when you first arrive in a different country. It's a new beginning. Everything is unfamiliar, and any direction you take brings about a new destination. Everywhere you look, you are surprised. You feel excited and confident at the same time, having achieved your goal; you feel on top of the world. One of the first things you might do is get some food, and because you're not on a holiday, you will most likely need to buy groceries. When you finally find the nearest supermarket, you'll realize you need to pay. Maybe you have cash, but it's not the same currency. It's Okay, you have your credit card and can pay with that.

So far so good, but you may also need extra furniture for the place you're renting, where you also need to leave a deposit. Then, you'll need a phone service, internet, TV, gas, electricity, etc.

How will you pay these initial payments? Do you have a local bank account? Can you open an account if you don't have a job yet? Can you open an account with your passport or will they request a local I.D.?

When you have just moved to a new country, one thing you can be sure of is that your finances will be under pressure. When you first consider moving abroad, it is very important to check your funds before diving in head first.

> *"Hong Kong diary: Day 1*
>
> *Public transport: Huge stations, tiny fares!*
> *Groceries: Twice the price! Water for lunch?*
> *Dinner with friends: Thrice the price, I need a drink…Alcohol: *jaw drops* Exorbitant.*
> *Stopping comparing prices to your home town: PRICELESS."*
> **– Natasha from the UK**

Some people can handle money struggles no sweat, but if you'd prefer to take one stressful item off your list when moving abroad, it's worth putting a little cash aside as an emergency fund, especially in the beginning when you're getting settled. It's a lot more challenging difficult if the coffers are empty.

Keeping a little on the side is also important for the extra travel you will probably be taking. The fact is that we, as expats, more often than not, are the ones having to go back to visit family and friends, as opposed to them visiting us. My mom is great in reminding me very gently: "Rachel, you are the one who chose to live abroad, not us." Just like me, many expats include one or more trips back home in their budget and schedule.

Even if you're not a big spender, try to save money and keep indulgences to a minimum. Travelers often end up spending more than they planned. Exploring your new home may include more frequent visits to coffee shops, restaurants, or grocery shopping trips to find more food in the new culture that is to your liking.

Another reason it's important to pad your savings is medical emergencies. An accident or sickness is never planned, no matter where you are in the world. But in a foreign country, it's very possible you'll have to rely on your funds to receive the care you need.

Regardless of emergencies, it's usually a good idea to open a local bank account in your new country, especially if you are working there. Having a local bank account will make your life a lot easier in terms of integrating. Bear in mind that every country has their own regulations for opening an account and most do require items such as an I.D., employer references, a utility bill, or rental contract. Often it can be rather frustrating as the forms and documents you need to read and sign are in a foreign language, and staff typically do not speak English, leading to misunderstandings, and a sense of insecurity and uncertainty.

For the vast majority of expats, these issues are minor and accepted as part of the journey. With experience, these early glitches and confusions become amusing stories to later be shared and laughed at with friends over a glass of wine. Yet for a newbie who isn't properly prepared, these initial irritations can set the tone for all future exchanges with their local banks, and become a situation of frustration and mistrust.

Tips on Banking

A few suggestions regarding bank accounts—first, asking locals for their recommendations provides an enormous help in deciding which bank you'll open an account with. This saves a lot of time researching the options, which we foreigners, can't really know without more real-life exposure. Before moving to any country, I always try to connect with locals, either by asking my future boss or colleagues by email, or by posting on expat forums for the country I'm moving to. I always prefer doing what the locals do over assuming because a bank has tellers who speak English, it must be the best bank.

Another important thing to remember is to ask how to cancel the account when you leave. This is a funny question to ask when you're looking to open an account and they're happy to have a new customer. However, keep in mind that moving out of your host country usually happens in less time, with less preparation than moving in. At a time when you have a long to-do list and little time, you'll be happy to know the procedure for canceling an account so you needn't spend extra time while you're packing up. Most banks allow you to do it online, which is easy if you remember who to email and what all the codes and numbers are.

This brings me to my last tip, which is to keep all your paperwork organized in a folder, without throwing much, or any of it away—even after you leave a country. I learned my lesson a full year after I said my goodbyes and moved on. I was carefully filling in my tax papers when they asked about my bank information for the previous year. "Oh no, what was the name of that French bank again? The banker's name was Christophe something. I had an online account, but where's that link and code?" From then on, I made sure I kept everything together, without any additional stress.

Keeping your existing bank account in your country of origin is usually a good idea. It helps to keep your credit facilities open while you are away, but also good in case you can't open a new account in your new country right away.

One time, I had opened a new account but they only allowed the minimum credit limit and since I had to buy new furniture, I reached my limit after buying a bed, a table and four chairs. My option could have been to wait a month for a couch, TV and kitchen supplies, but sitting on a chair and dining out every day is not my preference. Since I always keep my bank account in my country of origin, with a higher credit limit, I was able to relax at home with homemade food. This was one of the rare times I moved without furniture and couldn't find a decent furnished apartment, and in this case, had to dip into my emergency funds. It does happen sometimes!

Hidden Fees

And that brings us to foreign exchange rates and their fluctuations. The latter can have a big impact on your income as an expat, especially where large sums of money are involved. It is therefore something to take into account when accepting a job or considering a move. For example, you can usually request your salary is paid in the currency of the country where you will be living and working. This option often depends on if you're moving with your family or alone, and if you plan to stay for a longer or short-term contract. If you need to transfer money to your home country, you will hit the same issues.

The currency exchange rate is one of the potential pitfalls when working or living abroad. For many retires, this is often the breaking point and therefore important to bear in mind.

Follow the Logic

Discussing finances may be terrifying to some of you; however, to avoid panicking as you work your way through this book, simply take a moment and remember to BREATHE. Focus on your own current situation and start putting things in logical order. Who are you? What is your family situation? What is your reason for moving? How long do you plan on staying abroad? What is your destination?

Answering these key questions will help you realize where your focus should be with regards to each chapter and every checklist. Moments of panic are very normal, but I always prefer to have them beforehand, rather than in a foreign destination where you don't necessarily have the benefit of an existing support system.

Tips for Your Financial Planning:

Along with planning what to see and do when you move abroad, financial planning should not be forgotten. The below list can save you from potential problems down the line:

• **Notify your financial institutions**

Inform your home bank and credit card companies about where you will be traveling to, and the duration of your stay in the foreign country.

The slightest deviation from your normal spending habit can cause red flags and lead to blocking your account. If that happens, even your credit card might be denied. The information you provide before moving will prevent any of this awkwardness. Most banks allow you to do this online.

- **Set up online accounts**

Nowadays, most people have an online bank account which allows added convenience and security over your funds while traveling abroad. With an online account, you can easily stay on top of your balances and transfers.

Setting up automatic payments can also help you pay certain bills on time.

- **Have multiple forms of payment**

Depending on your destination and spending habits, it's a good idea to carry a variety of payment methods such as cash, debit cards, and credit cards. Make sure your credit, debit or prepaid cards are accepted in the country you plan to visit.

It might be helpful to have at least two bank accounts and credit cards, specifically ones accepted internationally, such as Visa and MasterCard.

- **Pay attention to safety**

Hopefully without sounding too much like a parent, please pay attention to keeping your cards, cash, and other documents in a safe place. For cash, the golden rule is never keep all your eggs (money) in one basket (your bag or wallet or pocket). If you are robbed or misplace your stuff, you'll have lost everything. With multiple cards, store your extra card locked away safely in your home. Avoid carrying valuables in places in pockets or bags that leave them easy for anybody passing to grab. This goes without saying in any place, anytime, anywhere, but it's especially important to stay alert in an unfamiliar environment.

- **Emergency phone numbers**

On the back of your card you'll see an emergency phone number to cancel the card if need be. Very handy when you lose your card, so keep this info written somewhere else, or save in the number your smartphone along with numbers for the local police, etc.

- **Check the exchange rates**

Familiarize yourself with foreign currency and exchange rates to understand their value. You can use an app, or even Google, to find out the current exchange rates, but it's helpful to get some practice in ahead of time. Instead of changing money at the last minute at the airport or abroad, you'll always find better rates if you plan in advance. There are several options for you to buy foreign currency (online, offline, from banks, from private retailers, or even friends), so research your options be-forehand.

- **Extra fees**

In addition to exchange rate conversion fees, you may encounter foreign exchange fees when transferring money abroad. Make sure you are aware of these.

- **Cash is king**

No one turns down cash. Carrying a couple hundred dollars or euros worth of emergency cash is a wise deci-sion. Picture yourself in a remote part of the world, on a dark, late night, ready to catch the last train before mid-night and your card is being swallowed by the ATM. This is a nightmare that can become reality unless you have cash to help you avoid this disaster. There are some placed where cash is the only option. In certain parts of Africa and Asia for example, the only money available is what you bring in. Just make sure to carry cash in small amounts, rather than showing large bundles of money in public. The challenge is keeping your money safe while you travel.

In summary, financial planning should not be forgotten in your preparation to move abroad. Besides the basics of taking your credit card and keeping some cash in your wallet, these suggestions and tips will further advance your preparation and keep your stress level at a minimum while avoiding potential obstacles.

KEY TAKEAWAYS:

→ Set some savings aside as emergency funds
→ Ask locals for bank recommendations and open a local account while also keeping your account back home
→ Plan and try to anticipate everything your budget might include
→ Keep your cards, cash, and other documents in a safe place.

Chapter 4
Reasons to Relocate

> *"Twenty years from now you will be more disappointed by the things you didn't do than by the ones you did do."*
> **–Mark Twain**

At only twenty-years-old, an ambitious young woman was running two businesses, soon building up a strong, consistent customer base. It was rewarding work for someone with a strong, entrepreneurial spirit, but after six years spent essentially working day and night, she found herself inspired by the idea of living life abroad. The idea came from her clients, who were mostly expats themselves, and bit by bit, she found herself longing for that experience too, traveling to a foreign country, learning about other cultures, learning new languages, and meeting new people. She couldn't let go of that dream so she decided to make it reality.

When we discuss reasons for moving, the above reasons were mine; I wanted to experience life in other places and explore other cultures. In essence, I didn't want to stay stuck in the same routine, work, house, and town for the rest of my life. I didn't want to feel like I was swimming in the same lane of a swimming pool for my entire life. I wanted to swim in the ocean amongst other fish in different colours and sizes. The ocean never gets boring.

Whether you need to work abroad or not depends on your reasons for relocating.

These reasons are the baseline for every step that follows. Without knowing your true intentions, it will be difficult to determine the path for your life abroad. Your destination might also be hard to determine without a clear goal. If you don't know why you want to leave your home town, how will you know what to do differently when you're gone?

> I came to the Netherlands for love. My husband is born and raised in the Netherlands and I was working in Indonesia at the time when we met in person (we're a product of the internet age). The decision to move here was purely for family. I wanted the kids to have roots and to be settled in an environment that they can call home. So work was not a priority at that time. I became immersed in the world of parenting and I love it."
> **– Lana from the Philippines**

> "I follow my husband wherever he goes! His job took us from Australia to Asia and now Europe. My impression is positive! Having said that, I must add that I hate cold and miss the warmth and the sun so much! "
> **– Joyce from Australia**

Driven to Relocate

The number of people living abroad has grown steadily over the past decade and will continue to increase as travel becomes easier, and more people become interested in exploring other languages and cultures, or finding a job abroad.

Exchange programs are wonderful opportunities to taste life abroad. On top of that, they can be sponsored by your university or a student exchange organization. Usually, students live at their parents' house, so all they need to do is pack up their suitcases and book their flight. It's a lot less stress and an amazing opportunity. If this is your situation, I have one word for you: GO!

As a student, your specific area of interest will determine the type of university you wish to attend, which also can narrow down possible destinations. A student visa would then be your next step.

If you're going for a language course, the duration of your trip would probably be short term. For example, France is an attractive country for those wanting to become more fluent *pour parler le Français*. You can mingle with the locals and enjoy some sightseeing while you're there. In this case, having some money put away would be necessary as your move abroad would be a spending trip rather than one spent earning a living.

Do you want to work as a volunteer? Finding a location to volunteer doesn't usually pose a challenge. The decision of where to go sometimes can however, because of the wide selection of options. Your choice will be based on your personal drive, likes, and desires. Your preferences

41

may lead you toward a warm climate, or maybe you wish to be surrounded by baby elephants, or help children in developing countries. There are many things to consider when choosing a place to volunteer.

If your objective is to have a job overseas, your existing skills and education are important for your job searches. Employment opportunities in your field will help determine destinations. Then comes applying for jobs and once accepted, the company can, in many cases, help you relocate and arrange the visa.

Thinking about why you want to move is essential in your preparation. For me, it meant I had to end two successful businesses and make sure I would have an income while living abroad. That's why I had to search for a job before moving, or else the financial risks would've been too high.

Have you ever heard the saying that the grass is greener on the other side?

Up to this point, we've covered the obvious reasons for moving. Now, it's time to dig somewhat deeper.

If you read the first chapter of this book, you've probably given some thought to what your personality is like and can now answer the less straight-forward questions about your desire to leave home. Why do you really want to move? To escape the rainy days? To launch a new career? To grow your confidence? To earn more money? To improve your CV? To gain independence or self-improve? To experience a new culture? To live more cheaply?

Do you think the work might be easier or more fun? Will the people be nicer? Will the food taste better? Will you have fewer bills to pay?

Is the grass really greener once you cross the border?

Please realize that moving abroad will not solve all the PROBLEMS you have in your home country. If your reason to leave is to escape from debts, you probably won't be able to hide forever. Things will pile up and get worse.

Another consideration are the long-term consequences of moving. If you are discussing a new job option, it's important to know exactly what you're getting into. Ask as many relevant questions as possible during your job interview to avoid surprises once you're at your destination. In addition to your new employer, you can reach out to your new colleagues and talk to them about the workplace and job. You'll get an immediate feel for the atmosphere, their helpfulness, and your new surroundings if you decide to take the job. This may be difficult if it's your first move, as it was in my case. I wasn't able to come up with the right questions during my first interviews, leading to surprises regarding working hours, lunch breaks, and workload. These days, during job interviews, I ask more questions than the person interviewing me. In fact, I enjoy job interviews so much, I encourage you to accept as many as you can, just for the experience, if nothing else!

Questions to ask your potential new employer:
- Where is the office located? What is it like?
- What else is nearby in the area?
- Is it safe/possible to walk outside alone?

- Is the office easy to reach by public transportation or by bike?
- What is the dress code?
- Am I able to ask my boss and/or colleagues questions directly?
- Can I work from home?
- Are the hours in the office flexible or do we all begin and end at the same time?
- Is it normal to work late nights and/or weekends?
- If I become ill, what is the procedure to call in absent?
- Who will pay for relocation expenses?
- What does the future of this company or position look like?

Knowing the answers to these questions will not only help you form an opinion about the job, but may also influence your decision to move.

Relocation can be a big risk, but sometimes big risks can equal big rewards, which is important to keep in mind.

If you feel stuck in your current job and don't feel your existing city offers the best opportunities, then you should seriously consider relocating. If you want to work in a specialized field that doesn't yield jobs in your hometown, you have a great reason to consider moving. If you're just ready for a change in your life and are open to new things, relocation may make you very happy.

Questions to ask yourself

As with the questions for a new employer, it's essential to ask yourself some important questions as well. The more you ask, the more self-aware you become, and being self-aware is being self-knowledgeable. It is the key to being successful in any area of your life from relationships, to career, to business and overall well-being. Especially when making a decision as big as moving abroad, it's crucial to understand what makes you tick.

The more you know about what is important to you, what motivates you, what your intentions and values are, the better choice you'll make. Some people think they can just wing it with regards to relocating for work and then the shock is huge when they arrive and can't adapt to the new neighbourhood. These people are usually the first to buy a ticket back home.

Questions to ask yourself before you relocate for a job include:

- Is the position one in which I can envision myself learning and advancing my career?
- What are the benefits of relocating for this job? Do they outweigh the obstacles?
- What is the cost of living in this new city? Can I afford to live in the new city and still save some money?
- Do I make friends easily?
- Will living and working in the new city provide me with better opportunities than my current situation?
- Is my partner/family supportive of this decision and where will he/she work?
- What are some activities I might enjoy in the new city outside of work?
- What and whom am I leaving behind? How does that feel?

- Do I tend to do well with change?
- Where will my kids go to school? Does the school have a good reputation?
- What is the neighbourhood like? Could I easily adjust to new surroundings?
- Is the climate one I can comfortably live in?
- What's my backup plan if things don't work out?
- Am I feeling excited about the idea of moving?

Ask yourself what you have to gain—and to lose—by relocating, and keep in mind that if it doesn't work out, you can always move back.

A Closer Look at Finding Work Abroad

If you aren't transferring with your current job, but are still planning to find work, ensure you tackle the issue of employment beforehand. Make sure you consider the following:

- If you're not being relocated by your current employer, it's best to start your job hunt well ahead of time, while you are still in your familiar home town.
- Decide if you really need or want to work abroad. If so, try to search within your current company or employment; it is to your advantage financially.
- Remember it usually takes longer than planned, and it can be rather difficult if you don't speak the language. Investigate the job market thoroughly before you leave home.
- Decide if you want short-term, seasonal, volunteer, or long-term employment.

- Apply for a work permit if needed.
- If you plan to start your own business, hire professional and legal support.
- Before signing any employment contract, pay extra attention to working hours, benefits, holidays, training, and other agreements as they may be very different from what you are used to.
- Jobs vacancies can be searched before moving on sites such as: LinkedIn, Indeed, Monster, Internations. Also consider consulting recruitment agencies or ask other expats for suggestions.
- Places to look for job postings after moving include: local schools or universities, bulletin boards (at hostels, supermarkets, or libraries), the embassy, local online searches (LinkedIn, Monsters, Indeed, Craigslist, etc.), temp agencies, and by word of mouth through your network.

More Job Ideas

Whether your goal is to travel and earn some money to continue your travel, or you want to explore a city for a longer time, you may want to consider these more casual careers:

- Language teacher: teach your native language at language centers and cultural associations abroad. English teaching jobs are popular and a TESOL/TEFL certification is all you need.
- Farm employee: help a farmer harvest fruit in Australia, pick olives in Spain, etc.

- Volunteering: help prepare for Carnival in Brazil, make jewelry out of seeds in Ecuador, assist at the health centers in India, collaborate on childcare projects in Cambodia, etc.
- Au pair: if you like being with children and you're under 30, you can stay with the host family for food and shelter and earn some extra spending money too.
- Waiter: a job you can find all over the world as you'll find bars, restaurants, hotels, cubs, and discos pretty much everywhere. If you dislike customer service, you can easily help in the kitchen, prepping food or washing dishes.
- Tourist guide: tour operators often seek staff to accompany groups and travelers.
- Cruise ship worker: there are many jobs to find on board: entertainment, sales, hospitality, restaurant, or tending bar. You may need to work many hours at a fast pace, but equally fast money will fill your pockets.
- Entertainer: organizing activities for guests at holiday resorts or hotels. Teach yoga or salsa, run a painting class, perform theatre, etc.
- Diving instructor: if you are a scuba diving expert, you can find these jobs in many different countries.
- If you are looking for a permanent, or at least longer stay abroad, you may prefer to have a more stable job. A book I enjoyed that includes helpful true stories and tips about making a living abroad is *Free at Last: Live, Love and Work abroad as a 21* by Kristen Palana and Jacqueline Seidel.

Based on your skills and education, you can start searching for jobs in your field. After crafting your C.V. and cover letter, you can begin to apply to companies in one or more destinations. I like to apply to a wide variety of countries without being picky about the location. The responses you receive can be seen as a sign that those are the places most suitable for you at that time in your life. Sometimes it's best to let the universe do its work and just trust how your life unfolds.

KEY TAKEAWAYS:

→ Figure out your real reason for moving: job, partner, escape, study, etc.

→ A clear reason to move makes every further step in the process easier

→ Self-awareness is a great tool for success

→ In times of homesickness, remember the reason you left and you're cured!

Chapter 5
Where in the World Will You Go?

If money was not an issue and you could live anywhere in the world, where would it be?

Ask someone randomly where they would like to live and you will hear all kinds of tropical-flavoured answers: "Oh, I would definitely go the Caribbean and lay on the beach, drinking a cocktail, and getting a nice tan. Or, I would go to Africa on a safari and enjoy the wild life. Or perhaps Hawaii because I've seen how beautiful it is on TV. Actually, New Zeeland is amazing too; the nature and waterfalls…"

Now imagine having to stay there for an undetermined time (at least a year). Would you enjoy being on an island for a whole year? Would you still enjoy laying on the same beach when hurricane season arrives? Would you enjoy the wild animals and nature if it meant giving up being near a city, a supermarket, and other shops for a long time?

Holiday destinations are fun, exciting, and pretty much no-brainer destination choices, easily decided on over coffee. But choosing a country with the intention of staying requires significantly more thought, and can take weeks, or even years. It's a huge step not to be taken lightly. Planning and research are crucial in your decision, and you'll notice those factors will be repeated in every chapter, because their importance cannot be stressed enough.

What Are You Hoping to Get Out of This?

Once you've made yourself aware of your reasons for moving, which we discussed in the previous chapter, the choice of location becomes somewhat easier. Please note the word, "somewhat".

In my case, my goal was to live abroad and stay there for an undefined length of time. That's why I wanted to secure an income there to minimize financial risks. Basically, I knew I needed to find a job abroad in advance and it took me a year to prepare and decide on the country I would move to. Most time consuming was the job application process, but all that effort started paying off when I received job offers in Curacao, London, Monaco, and Mallorca, Spain. Then I travelled to all those countries to check out each opportunity and gain a better sense of what each area had to offer. After weighing my options, I decided on Mallorca, Spain as my first destination abroad.

The choice you're making here is not if, but where you'll move to. Even after countless hours of research, there will always be many factors you can only understand once you experience them at your destination. Think about the fresh, pure air of the Swiss mountains compared to the smog hanging over Beijing. You can't really know what that's like until you take a deep breath right then and there.

> *"My fiancée and I both wanted to move out of Greece, that was certain, and it had to be Europe, for family and distance reasons. While being an Erasmus student in Brussels, Belgium, back in 2006, I had the chance to travel to Netherlands, and was amazed by the atmosphere, people, architecture, welcoming people, and landscape. So, my decision to choose NEDERLAND was quickly made!"*
> **- Laertis from Greece**

The Magic of a Discovery Trip

Often, a preliminary trip to check out the country you are considering is a wise choice and one I've made with every country I've lived in. If you move only for a temporary study or work up to a year, it is less essential than for a long-term move. Getting a sense of the daily life in your host country will really help you in your decision. When I had a job offer in Curacao, I was so excited to move to the Caribbean, I imagined all the wonderful aspects about it: blue skies, warm climate, colourful houses, beaches nearby, people smiling all the time…

Then I went on a trip to check it out and reality hit me. Warm climate? Yes, but really hot weather every single day started to feel exhausting. Beaches? Yes, but the beaches nearby were also the borders of the island. I realized how small it was, even somewhat claustrophobic. I talked to the locals and they admitted that after a while one can get pretty tired of the limitations of an island. Every time you want to leave, you need to take a plane. Sure, it can be done, but for even a quick, short getaway, you take a plane. The cost starts to add up. I also noticed all the plugs were different. Of course, they have different electricity—some places do—but I never thought about it until I was there. All my appliances wouldn't be useable, not without adaptors. And what about the people smiling all the time? Yes, there was some of that. But when I went to investigate my job offer, people didn't seem happier there than in the job I had at home. Sometimes hard work needs to be done, no matter where you are.

I was so happy I went to visit and felt so good to say "no, thank you" to the job offer. I have no regrets. The same thing happened with my decision regarding a job located in Monaco, France. Awesome place when you see it on TV. Huge yachts and famous people, and I would get to work there! I couldn't wait! Until I went to visit and found out how expensive it is to live there. Renting is unaffordable, so you need to live outside Monaco, commuting in daily.

Bottom line, a short trip can go a long way toward helping you make your decision. When you visit your potential future home, take the time to research essentials such as housing, banking, grocery shopping, transportation, and the cost of living. Visit an agency to find out about houses for rent, their prices and whether they're furnished or not. Ask them what you need to do for utilities and how to get a telephone and internet access.

Imagine living there, not just visiting. Talk to locals, find people in the area so you can get a feel for the neighbourhood you will be in every single day. Look at the distances to commercial areas, your work, a school, the airport, and the city center. If you like sports or enjoy going out clubbing, find out about the selection of gyms, sport clubs, discos, and nightclubs nearby. If you play music, enjoy singing, or dancing, or reading, make sure you check out the libraries, studios, and theaters.

Last but not least, pay attention to your gut feeling. Does it feel awkward and uncomfortable or does the environment make you smile and lift your mood? It's actually those small details, those fine daily habits that we often miss when we're abroad. Moving overseas is a drastic change, that's why finding the activities you love most are crucial to making you feel at home in no time.

While taking this discovery trip, it's good to talk to locals and get an idea of the culture. Are the local people easy to talk to and make contact with? If you don't speak the language, are they adjusting to speaking English with you? For example, when I arrived in Spain, I only spoke a little Spanish and the locals were not using much English at all. However, the contact went surprisingly well with a mix of *Spanglish* and hand gestures; it was actually great fun and I felt so welcome. On the other hand, in France, even though I spoke French, I felt like a stranger for months as nobody seemed to make any effort to get to know me. Knowing this beforehand, you may consider taking language lessons before you move. Communication is crucial to your integration, which you'll read about in the following chapter.

Sometimes the people were the determining factor in my *feel-good* decision, and other times, it was the environment. You can't expect to find 100% of all your desires, but there has to be some type of *gut feeling* before you decide.

If you can find any expatriate organizations or groups, it's good to contact them so you can talk to others who have been living there. They can share insights as outsiders, such as the hardest cultural differences to adjust to, or the biggest obstacles you'll probably face. Their information can be very valuable in your decision-making process.

The longest period I've spent on my discovery trips is one week, but depending on your available time and budget, you can choose to extend your trip.

After your exploration trip, you'll need some time to reflect and absorb all your impressions. One thing I learned from making impulsive decisions, which I often regretted the next day, is to never jump to conclusions right away. Always sleep on it first. It took me years to realize how valuable this advice is and more years to put it into practice. Once you've been there, you can take another look at your current life, your routines, preferred habits, and start to consider if you can either do similar activities abroad, or if not, can you easily let go of your habits and create fresh ones? After some time, if everything still feels positive and exciting, you're probably in a good place to make your final decision.

Matching Your Destination to Your Purpose

To pick the perfect destination, I highly recommend you take into account your personal interests, and educational or career goals. If you are a globetrotter and you like the adventure, you can take your backpack and look for local, informal jobs that will earn enough for you to continue your travel. If you are seeking a place to retire, you will be looking for somewhere to stay permanently, but your options will depend on your savings, so make sure you check out the cost of living in your preferred destinations.

If you are working and your company relocates you, they probably have a specific job and location ready for you, a choice for you to either take or leave. A simple yes or no is all that's required. But what if you're relocating by yourself? If you're looking for a job abroad, and are open to several regions, then the first step is to look for vacancies that match your skills. This will help you identify your best options. Finding a job was always my top priority when deciding where to live.

Some may say that being single is so much easier. I've heard all kinds of comments: "You're single, you can go anywhere you want. And you have nobody else to look after or provide for. You're free and it's so easy for you to move." These comments used to irritate me, because as a single, making every decision alone is not fun. Brainstorming important decisions with yourself is like turning around in circles and always passing by the same thoughts. Moving abroad with all the packing, unpacking, carrying around luggage and decorating a house is definitely easier if you're not alone. How often have I sat on the floor holding a screwdriver in one hand and a wooden shelf in my other hand, to then realize I can't possibly hold two vertical sides together and fit the shelf, alone!

Or think about the moving company loading everything off, which I need to unpack, but at the same time, I need to be in my new job daily (remember I need to earn my own income), and let the movers in, and make an appointment for the utilities etc....

Anyway, I stopped answering those comments as

there's no point in arguing it. One thing I do answer is that whether you are single, married, retired, young, or older, every situation has its advantages and disadvantages. All I focus on is my own position, which is challenging enough. Look at your own needs and wants and make sure you seek what's best for you.
toward

Consider the Economic and Political (In)stability

Regardless of your destination, it's important to investigate the economic conditions of your new home. The currency can be much stronger or weaker, impacting your financial situation as mentioned in the chapter about finances. These factors should not be your only consideration, but seeking an affordable destination might be a higher priority if you are a student or volunteer as you won't receive a fixed, regular paycheck. As an expat, and foreigner, you are usually part of the larger socio-economic group and are able to shop in the same stores and go to the same markets as the locals; however, you could very well be part of a small group on a completely different socioeconomic plane than most locals. In that case, wealthier expats tend to live in guarded compounds, and often go to completely different stores than the locals. They also hardly ever interact with the local population due to the large income gap. But being part of the economic elite, makes you more vulnerable to theft, violent crime, or even terrorist attacks. Fortunate with a fortune?

Next to the economic situation, the political climate is an important point of interest as well. Do some reading on the country's history and find out about any recent civil war or other conflict. Is the government in control? Sometimes elections can lead to changes in power, resulting in riots and chaos. Would such changes put you and your family in danger? Is there any anti-American, anti-Western, or anti-Asian sentiment that might impact your stay? Developing countries for example, may have unstable governments, which sometimes fail to provide basic services to its citizens. It's worth doing some research before your final decision.

Living in a socially, economically, and politically stable country will make your stay overseas much easier and more pleasant. Keep in mind that the majority of expats end up being very satisfied and dangers are rare. The reason to research and read is there to ensure you pick the place that's right for you so you can join the satisfied majority of expats.

You will most likely be treated with greatest respect and hospitality on one crucial condition, which is to travel responsibly when living abroad. In other words, always show respect for your hosts in a host country.

Check the Price of Milk

Let's take a closer look at the cost of living within a country. Would you expect New York or Dubai to be the priciest places to live? You might be surprised by the answer when you do a search for the most expensive cities for expats. Several studies show settling in a developing country can be rather costly. With a simple online search, you can find the most accurate surveys that rank cities worldwide depending on the cost of living for expatriates. Additionally, you can find comparison sites that calculate the differences in cost of living between cities of your choice. (Search for keywords: compare cost of living index) Read through these as part of your research to find out which are the world's costliest cities before relocating.

If you do your research, you can avoid big surprises down the road. It will also help you calculate the funds you would need to get started.

Questions to ask regarding the cost of living:

- How much will you earn?
- What is the cost of food staples (bread, eggs or milk)?
- How much of your budget will go toward housing (rent, utilities, etc.)?
- What is the cost of clothing (jeans, shoes, etc.)?
- What is the cost of personal care (medicine, deodorant, shampoo, etc.)?
- What is the cost of entertainment (movie tickets, gym, dining out, etc.)?
- What is the cost of transportation (gas, taxi, bus, etc.)?

The Unknown or the Familiar?

Another way to narrow your choice and facilitate your selection between countries is to considering places that already interest you, or perhaps places where you've enjoyed a vacation. Try to think of those regions that left a lasting impression, or the countries that had the right *feel*. Ideally, you will desire your new residence to offer you the incredible sense that it is where you belong, a place you can call home, and where you will find a lasting happiness. Very often, the immaterial can weigh out the material or tangible reasons. This is true for the country, as well as the actual house you'll choose within your region.

One time, I chose a tiny apartment over a spacious, luxurious one, just because of the amazing view of the beach. Watching the ocean, hearing the waves and simply having that serenity to wake up to and admire every day, was most important factor for me.

Some of you may have friends or family already settled abroad, which can determine your selection. Returning to your familial roots can be a reason to favor the country of your ancestors. This will also probably give you some level of familiarity with the culture.

On the other hand, a fair number of individuals adore the unknown. Those who embrace a completely new environment, whether it's a tropical rainforest, or amongst the wildlife of Africa.

The proximity to your home country may be an important factor for you too. If you like to visit your family and friends on a regular basis, and you decide on a far-away host country, would you be prepared to take a boat, a train, and two flights to get there? Maybe living there is very cheap, but the long-distances flights can be really expensive and time consuming.

And of course, your feelings on a given location are very subjective. I know many people who are very satisfied living in places I would never choose for myself. The entire process is quite personal, and often unique for each of us. Moving between European countries and North America is not as huge a challenge as, say, moving to China, because you'll find several similar cultural traits. Think about eating from your own individual plate with a fork and knife compared to using chopsticks and sharing dishes.

All of this may feel somewhat overwhelming. Just remember, this is exactly why you are preparing yourself well by doing your homework beforehand. Full and proper planning includes the looking within yourself, your own family situation, your reasons, your finances, your wishes and desires—all of that will help you on your journey.

KEY TAKEAWAYS:

→ Use your reasons for moving abroad to brainstorm a list of possible destinations
→ Immerse yourself in the magic of a discovery trip before your final decision
→ Consider the economic and political situation, the cost of living, and other
→ aspects you're not accustomed to
→ Take plenty of time to thoroughly consider your options

Chapter 6
Accommodation

I'M SO EXCITED!!"
At this point, you've made the decision to move abroad and chosen your destination. *"YEAH!"*
The moving date is finally getting closer, but then you remember you still need to find a place to live.
"OH NO!"

Finding a suitable home in a new country plays a significant role in integrating and settling in as expats. You want to find yourself a nice place where you feel comfortable and can easily fall asleep at night. You could choose to stay in a hotel at first, but in addition to the high cost, it's not common or ideal long-term. Many expats tend to book a hotel the only first week or month before moving into their new accommodations. And this is often due to furniture traveling somewhat slower than the person who needs it.

Generally speaking, expats will choose to either rent or buy accommodations, and these two routes will be the main focus of this chapter. I should mention there is a small portion of expats who don't belong to these two groups. They are either the ones who already have a property abroad and can move right in upon arrival, or students who receive student housing, or volunteer workers who are offered food and boarding in exchange for hours of work.

Those in the first category, who will rent, will either have to arrange it themselves or, depending on their work situation, may receive the support of their employer.

Those in the second group who intend to buy a new property once they arrive may choose to first stay in rented accommodations while searching for their new house.

Whichever your situation is, finding a place to live that feels right to you is one of the most important decisions you have to make as an expat. It's where you will have your private space, your safe haven, where you can rest or do whatever you want. In other words, it is your new home.

When you're finally finished unpacking all your boxes and have found a good place for every piece of furniture, it's usually with the intention to stay for a longer while. Research has shown that moving home is one of the top stressors in life, more stressful than a relationship breakdown, divorce or even a new job. Even if you upgrade from a small cottage to a palace, and you are extremely happy about your move, it disrupts your (and your family's) routine completely. In fact, dealing with disorganized possessions and realizing old favourite furniture doesn't fit in the new house tops the list of most stressful moving day moments. Many people even admit leaving things weeks before unpacking all the boxes. A different experience for each of us, but definitely not usually a seasonal routine.

Should You Rent Out Your Current Home?

Before you do anything else, you need to think about what to do with your current situation. If you are still living in your parents' house, you have a huge advantage over others. This entire step can be deleted from your list, because your house will remain nicely warm and cozy after you leave and there's no need to resign from any utility contracts. You can move on to the next steps.

If you own your home, you will need to think carefully about the different options for the time you are away. If you really need the money, or you don't intend to return to your house, putting it up for sale is an option. On the other hand, if money is not your biggest concern, renting out your property provides you with a major advantage with the security of having somewhere to live in case you need to return home sooner than expected. You never know what can happen.

If you decide to rent out your home while you are abroad, it is recommended you hire a real estate agent or use the services of a property manager. Different words are used to describe these agencies, but they can help you sort out everything from finding good tenants to ensuring your house is cared for while you focus on your new life abroad. This will give you the peace of mind knowing a professional is taking good care of everything. Whilst this comes at a fee, usually about 5-10% of the monthly rent, they will also attempt to keep it rented on a continuous base, which in turn helps cover other costs you have, such as mortgage payments.

Another option is to do it all yourself and try advertising to rent out your home, but remember you will be abroad and someone needs to deal with house visits, contracts, occasional repairs or maintenance, administration, etc.

Alternately, if you don't want to rent your house, consider asking a friend or relative to check on the house regularly, to keep it above freezing temperature, but also ventilated and damp-free. You probably need to keep your utilities connected, in order to leave the heating on at a minimum, and if you have a yard or garden, it will have to be maintained as well.

Should You Sell Your Current Home?

Many people choose to sell their property in order to receive the immediate funds they can then use to reinvest abroad. While that is a great thought, on the practical side, the timing is usually very hard to coordinate, as you may not be able to sell before your actual moving date.

The solution to this scenario is once again to hire a professional agent to handle the sale for you while you're gone. Besides this extra fee, you also don't know how long it will take before you receive your capital.

Before making such a major decision, you should at least consider that maybe after some months abroad, you could possibly decide that you don't like it. If that should happen and you have sold your house, you'll need to get back into the real estate ladder. This can be rather difficult, especially if you're already disappointed in having to repatriate. Therefore, it's worth postponing the sale for a while, and renting it out initially, until you test out the waters of your new life abroad.

> *"We discussed the idea of moving abroad during our honeymoon. Three years later, after being accepted into a volunteer organization that places people throughout Southeast Asia, we bought one-way tickets to Phnom Penh and said goodbye to our lives in the USA. We sold our large home and moved into a small condo. Right before moving, we sold our cars, closed down bank accounts and every other account we had, sold or gave away most of our possessions, and put the stuff we cared about into a storage unit where it is today. The hardest part was saying goodbye to our cat and we wouldn't talk about it for months as it upset us too much. Eventually, we found a home for her with one of our friends but it was really upsetting leaving her behind. When I went back to visit her later, she was so happy in her new home, and didn't even care that much about seeing me again!"*
> **- Gabi, British growing up in South Africa**

Renting or Buying Abroad

This choice is ultimately one that only you can make, but I hope the following thoughts will help you with your decision. Planning for your accommodations will include consideration of various factors such as the purpose and duration of your move as well as your destination and job. Whether you decide to rent or buy property abroad, in both cases there are some general guidelines to consider. First, it is wise to put time and effort into seeing the property in person instead of solely viewing it over the internet. Also, even if you know people in the new country who are offering their help, consider the services of an objective advisor who is experienced in that particular country's rules and regulations and who speaks the local language professionally. It's helpful to ask fellow expatriates already living in your target destination to recommend a local real estate agent.

Another thing to consider is your flexibility toward a new home. You may move from a rural area to a crowded city, where your only options will be apartments instead of houses. You may need to adapt to accommodations with less overall space, smaller rooms, in a louder neighbourhood, etc. Or, vice versa, you may move to a bigger house, surrounded by nature, with the sound of birds waking you every morning, and spacious rooms that are well cared for by your new domestic help.

"Having a support group here in terms of live-in help, that's what I call benefits. It allows me to create more space inside my mind, so I can focus better on what I need to do."
- Marc, American living in Malaysia

Buying Property Abroad

When you decide to buy, begin by hiring a professional advisor, experienced in regulations for non-residents, and who is not related to the real estate agent or owner of the property, and who communicates in your language as well as the local language. It's complicated enough to begin with, but every country has different laws, costs, and procedures, so asking for legal help is definitely not superfluous before making a decision.

The following tips are similar to ones you'd follow when buying property in your home country, but are still very important to consider:

- Visit the property on several occasions and during various times of the day
- Ensure the neighbourhood fits your needs
- Pay attention to the noise from neighbours, traffic outside, trains nearby, etc.
- Consider the different seasons: isolation in case of heavy winter conditions, heavy storms, or rain. Inform about moisture, ventilation, etc.
- Additional costs may arise such as registration fees or when a property has several owners, additional fixed costs can include gardening, cleaning, maintenance, etc.
- Check accessibility of the roads nearby as well as public transportation
- Never sign any papers or contract that you don't understand, especially in a foreign language
- Always "sleep on it" before making a rushed decision, even if you think it's your dream house. One night allows a cool down of emotions.
- Have your property evaluated by a specialist to ensure some kind of independent valuation certificate is given that indicates any problems or defects. Nobody wants to become the own-

er of a property to find out after signing the papers that it's going to cost a fortune to fix or maintain or even be potentially unsafe to live in.

- Arrange your finances, bank necessities, and mortgage.
- Remember that the asking price is not your final amount to pay. Notary fees, real estate commission, taxes, insurance, etc., must all be added to the final bill, and can easily add up to 17% of the price.
- Beware that most older properties look amazingly epic on the outside but usually need a lot of renovation and restoration. Also regarding safety regulations, they don't comply as the modern rules were nonexistent back in the day. The budget to restore can often be higher than initially expected.

Renting Property Abroad

Many people consider renting a waste of money. "You throw away your money every month and you'll never own the place," is something I heard very often in different kind of ways. It's true, but moving into a new place, in a new country, with new people of a new culture, well, I must admit I happily rented everywhere I landed initially. It is a sensible approach and allows some kind of relief and peace of mind that "if" it doesn't work out, you can just pack your bags and move again. Either back home or to another area in your new country. You will not be the first and certainly not the last to do so.

Searching for a rental is not complicated at all these days thanks to the internet. You can find numerous websites from real estate agents and landlords in any country anywhere in the world. The most difficult part is deciding on the area you want to live in before you start your actual property search. Even if you have a job, that doesn't mean you want to live next door to your office. There are many other aspects playing a role, such as the safety of the neighbourhood, public transport nearby or easily accessible by car, noise, proximity of a city and shops, etc.

Just like buying, it is always recommended that you spend some time in the area before deciding.

Before contacting a professional, it's best you take a look around online, not only to gain an idea of what kind of accommodations to expect, but also so you can be more specific when you speak with a local estate agent to discuss your needs, wishes, and preferences. Searching online, you can choose a rental website with listings specific to your new country. After you decide between an apartment, house, townhouse, sublet, or single rooms for rent, you will be able to narrow your search criteria even further: furnished or unfurnished, short term or long term, holiday/summer rentals, ones that do or don't allow pets, etc.

Conducting your own search online will give you an immediate overview of what you can expect in that country. This is where geographic differences come into the picture. Different countries can have very different standards of living so be aware of this when looking around at houses. Even if you talk to an agent that tells you everything is included or everything is fine, that might not be the case by your standards. It's not necessarily that they're lying, it's that "fine" to them may include an electricity outage several times a week and the cellar routinely flooding two or three times per year!

We all grow accustomed to our own cultures, but when we move, we realize our idea of comfort might be very different from someone else's. When I moved to France I wanted a furnished apartment and thought finding out would be so easy and straightforward until I asked the real estate agent and he thought I was joking. "*Quoi? Un appartement meublé?*" I repeated my same request and then he said he could find me a furnished place if I live by the beach as they have rentals for tourists on a weekly basis—at very high price. The other option was to look in the city of Paris. Well, I needed a rental about a four-hour drive from Paris, so that was not an option for me. Back to square one. I adapted my requirements to "non-furnished". However, the shock I received was still huge when I visited the first potential apartment. I entered the so-called "kitchen" but there was no kitchen! It was an empty room to which the agent said, "You have to install your own kitchen of course." I soon learned that kitchens come in various forms: *cuisine* simply means the room used as kitchen, nothing else. It's pretty much a bare room without any built-in cupboards or electric units, and just a faucet sticking out of the wall. The upgrade to that is the *cuisine aménagée*, which is a kitchen equipped with built-in cupboards but without electric units. And finally, the *cuisine* équipée is a kitchen equipped with built-in cupboards and some electric units, which is the kind I wanted all along. Clearly my idea of a "kitchen" is not similar to that of the French.

Another interesting, yet very confusing, example showing cultural differences with regard to accommodations can be found in the Netherlands. Here you can make a selection between unfurnished, semi-furnished, soft-furnished, and fully furnished. "*What?*" Exactly my question when I first landed there. Generally, most apartments are rented out unfurnished, which means, no curtains, no lamps, no wall or floor coverings, and a kitchen with no appliances. This way, tenants can decorate, paint, choose carpet, whatever they personally like. Yet, this is very time-consuming and expensive and usually for those who enjoy DIY (Do It Yourself) projects. Clearly not my preference with my two left hands.

Then there are semi-furnished, or soft-furnished rentals, which may include wall and floor coverings, curtains, (ceiling) lights, a kitchen with appliances, and sometimes even a washer/dryer. All you need to bring is your own non-fixed furniture. Lastly, the furnished rentals have everything furnished, including decor, kitchen equipment, pots and pans, cutlery, plates and glasses, a TV, towels, bed linens, etc. However, always ask what is included or not, because it may seem complete and wonderful when you visit, yet things disappear once you actually move in.

When you are ready to speak with an agent, it is important to provide clarity about what you want and not just settle for any rental. You can specify how many bedrooms you would like, if you prefer detached or semi- detached, a house or apartment, furnished or not, whether you'd like a garden or garage, and perhaps most importantly, you can outline your budget. For me, my priority was to move as quickly and easily as possible. That meant an apartment that had at least a kitchen with appliances, a bathroom, a floor (not concrete) and lights.

Based on your specifications, the agent can make a list of possible rentals and then arrange visits for you. In every country, I asked them to plan a full day with 5 to 10 visits, after which I committed myself to decide without requesting more visits. I learned that there are rarely huge differences, and once you've seen a few, you get a fairly clear picture of what's out there.

More to consider when renting abroad:

- Visiting the rental more than once during different times of day can help you make new discoveries.
- Try to negotiate for a lease that matches your planned length of stay in the country. Or, you can also try to arrange for a short-term contract initially, which allows you to move later if you decide to.
- Rental agreements and rules vary immensely between countries and you should always research what the standard rules and procedures are in your new country before signing anything. Or hire a legal advisor. Beware of landlords or agencies who might advantage of your perceived lack of local knowledge.
- Ensure you know how much notice you need to give to the landlord before you leave. That way you don't end up paying an extra three months if you need to leave suddenly. It happened to me in Germany, where three months of notice is the standard.
- Check if the utilities are already connected in your new home, or what needs to be done to arrange the connection. Often, you need to search for, choose, and contact electricity

companies yourself, as well as gas, TV, internet, and telephone services. You can ask the locals or other expatriates for recommendations, or check comparison websites.

- Find out whether the water is safe to drink straight from the tap.
- Find out how they collect the garbage and if they have recycling programs in place.

Here's an overview of things to consider when looking for a suitable home in your new country:

- If you are **currently a home owner,** make a decision about your current property: will you sell it, rent it, or just leave it empty to be cared for by friends or family?
- If you decide to **rent out your current property**, decide if you want to take care of the process yourself or employ an estate agent to manage it for you. Think about the price, the utilities, the contract duration, and the repair and maintenance while you're gone. Be sure to consider all the administrative tasks, including legal paperwork.
- If needed, arrange for any **utilities** to be disconnected and cancel your existing utility payments and contracts. When renting, remember to give proper notice. Cancel other contracts and memberships, e.g. gym membership, internet, newspaper, etc.
- Regarding your **property abroad,** make a decision about buying vs. renting and what type of accommodations you are looking for, such as an apartment or a large family home.

The answer may depend on the reason for your relocation and whether you are moving abroad for a fixed term or indefinitely.

- **Whether you will be renting or buying**, list your requirements for your new home e.g. number of bedrooms, available parking, a garden, etc., as well as those for the location of your new home e.g. type of neighbour-hood, proximity to work, schools, shops, public transport, etc.

- Use the **internet** to research the property market in your new host city or country to find out what the options are, including costs.

- Arrange for **temporary accommodations**, such as a hotel or rental if you cannot move in upon arrival. Take into account the extra cost of this.

- If you **purchase** a property abroad, make sure you are familiar with all relevant legislation concerning property purchases by foreigners. Also consider all the available options, such as new builds, renovated houses, resale through estate agents or private sellers, self-build, etc. Ask experts about any risks involved and ask about the experiences of others by talking to expats in web forums.

- **If renting**, decide whether you wish to move into a **fully, semi-, or non-furnished** property.

- If possible, try to **visit** the area you are considering moving to and look at it during different times of day. Try to talk to the neighbours and get a feel for the area.

- Even with extensive Google searches, a good **real estate agent** is an invaluable resource. These agents have a good understanding of the local property market and can assist you in finding a home that meets all or most of your needs.

- When scheduling your move, if possible, make arrangements for the **utilities** (electricity, gas, water, internet) to be connected a day before you are due to arrive in case there are any last-minute problems or delays.

- Always consider the **safety and security** aspects of your new home. Thieves have a preference for expat homes because they hope to take advantage of your lack of your inexperience.

KEY TAKEAWAYS:

→ Renting or buying—consider both options carefully before deciding.

→ Visit properties in person, in addition to conducting internet searches.

→ Be on the lookout for property fraud or scams, whether at home or abroad.

→ A good real estate agent is invaluable in assisting you locally, legally, and with any other information you require.

Chapter 7
Speak the Local Language

> *"If you talk to a man in a language he understands,
> that goes to his head. If you talk to him in his own
> language, that goes to his heart."*
> **–Nelson Mandela**

"Parlo un poco Espanol."

My first words upon my arrival in Spain. Not too bad huh? Luckily, I knew more words and phrases than, "I speak a little Spanish", but I learned even more while I was living there. Many people move abroad thinking, "Oh, I'll be fine. I know a few Spanish words but mostly English. I'm sure they'll understand me." But then you step outside the airport into the local atmosphere, and suddenly all you hear is: *aqui, si, por favor, señor, que, a donde vas...*

"Wait, the whole world doesn't at least kind of speak English?"

No, they don't.

If this is a surprise to you, please continue reading. Upon arrival, you need to register in the town hall, get your residence ID, pick up your rental agreement, open a bank account, and of course, hook up all your utilities. In most of these transactions, you won't hear much English, or certainly not enough. Also, several companies, such as electricity, gas, telephone, or internet, will need to be reached by phone. Making a call in a foreign language is so much harder than speaking face-to-face, as you can't use hand gestures or facial expressions. Check the local language or potential for English in your host country and do your homework before you leave. Languages could be the least of your worries before you leave, but you could end up regretting that lack of knowledge enormously.

Learning a language is THE biggest challenge for many expats, hands down. In every interview I've done with expats, the last question I always ask is: what is your biggest tip for anybody moving abroad? You can probably guess the answer by now: learn the local language! In every conversation, both online and off, this is definitely a hot topic among expats. Whether I ask about their biggest challenge, or best advice, funny story, or the worst experience, the answer, in 90% of the cases, will always involve language.

Conversing is undoubtedly one of my favourite topics. As a polyglot or multi-linguist, whatever you want to call it, I speak six languages, teach half of them and am learning yet another. One thing is for sure, I truly adore languages and enjoy motivating others to learn because it enriches your life to a great extent.

You don't have to be an expat to benefit from this valuable knowledge. On the contrary, on a daily basis, I encounter situations where I pleasantly use a variety of jargon. Think about the global world we are living in—

your own neighbours might speak a foreign tongue, which you can then speak. At the airport, you can contact many more people, or you can sit on a bench, observe others, listen to other families or couples' discussions and fully understand what they are talking about. How fun is that? I've personally met so many people while waiting at the airport, and built relationships all over the world this way. Also, at work, or at conferences which include attendees from many cultures, you can be the one grasping everybody's conversations. At universities, exchange students, coming from abroad, are no longer exceptions, so whether you are studying in your home country or not, you can make friends or have relationships with peers speaking a language that deviates from your mother tongue.

> *"I turned on the local TV all the time, and watched Dutch soaps for hours and hours. I also went to the pub and that's where I learned the chit-chat-bar-language! But that brought me much closer to the locals! It helped me enormously and in a few months, I felt integrated!!"*
> **- Russel from the UK**

Adding Culture to the Mix

The importance of learning a local language is, especially for an expat, as important as learning about other cultures. If you speak the local tongue, it's easier to connect with the local people and understand them.

To better understand the importance of practicing languages in a foreign country, I refer you to this brilliant

81

quote from Rita Mae Brown: "Language is the road map of a culture. It tells you where its people come from and where they are going."

Cultural awareness and language proficiency go hand in hand. There's no two ways about it.

In every country I've lived, I'm grateful to learn a great deal about the culture. But this could never have happened if I didn't speak the local languages, even considering the fact that I'm very social and like to talk and meet people. In the UK, I met neighbours who taught me about typical English food and beers. In Spain, I learned about the three-course menu for lunch: *primero*, *secondo*, *è postré*, and I started practicing the afternoon power nap: *la siesta*.

In France, there are 101 regions called, *departements,* and amazingly there are differences in each with regard to greetings, dialect, accent, even food habits.

One common social minefield is knowing how and when to appropriately use *tu* or *vous'*. Both mean "you" in English, but not knowing when to use the formal *vous* or the informal *tu* can lead to some tricky situations. The distinction between *vous* and *tu* regards your relationship to the person you are talking to. *Tu*, when used inappropriately, can be interpreted as a lack of respect by certain people. That's why it's critical to know when to use *tu* and when to use *vous*. *Vous* is usually the safest bet. Nobody will ever blame you for being too formal. Pay attention to the moment someone says, "*tu peux me tutoyer.*" that's your ticket to safely switch to *tu* and keep at it. Good luck!

There are many further examples along these lines, but the same idea is at their core: immersing yourself in a culture is all about being able to understand cultural beliefs, core values, and behaviours, which you can only truly grasp by speaking the language. A culture is like an iceberg, the tip above the water is visible to everybody, but what's below is a much larger portion and invisible to the eye. Culture is so much more than the observable characteristics of a group, such as their food, music, arts or greetings. True understanding of a culture comes from the deeper components; below the water line, you'll find their complex ideas, preferences, typical behaviours, and values.

English Can Get You Anywhere and Nowhere

While English is pretty much common throughout the world, the extent to which it's understood and spoken varies tremendously. Also, sometimes people will tell you their English is good, while in practice, it's only about as good as my Chinese, which, at this point, I can only write 10 characters and say about 20 broken sentences. In some countries, where the level of English is low or non-existent, you will soon find the language barrier to be a big obstacle in your day-to-day life.

It is no longer a surprise that other expats' most common tip to those planning a move abroad is to learn the language. Undoubtedly, you'll read this in every expat's guide or interview or blog.

Home Sweet Home

"I feel at home!" is a sentence with a lot of meaning. Feeling at home means you feel truly comfortable and integrated wherever you are, even if it's not your native country.

I always say, "my home is where I live," and luckily, I've felt home everywhere I've been. And when that feeling disappears, I start planning my next move. If you are able to attempt conversation with the local people, you will have a much better chance of integrating and feeling more at home.

Whether you talk to intercultural specialists, read expat guides, or hear from other expats throughout the world, they would all agree that by understanding your host country's language, you will better understand the culture and customs of the people. Furthermore, learning a foreign language will increase your confidence level and help you to feel more at home. Vice versa, by feeling more at home, you will gain more confidence and become a happier person.

If you are moving abroad, having some knowledge of the local language in advance can help you find a place to live in your new destination before you arrive. Knowing an address to go to saves you another stressor when you land, as you can drive straight to your new place to unpack and avoid nights at a hotel. I've contacted real estate agents several times beforehand and when their English is not brilliant, there's simply no way to clearly communicate what kind of house or apartment you're looking for. If your requirement is to have your house close by the beach or highway, the meaning of *close by* can range from a one minute walk to a thirty-minute drive. Also, the meaning of highway might be *narrow sand roads* in some cultures. Once I asked for the beach and when I got there, it was a tiny shore, dirty and impossible to walk on let alone lay down. You couldn't even get to the water. But hey, the lady merely said it was the beach—she didn't say it was paradise!

Communication Barriers

A basic level of communication can help you deal with problems in various awkward situations. Think about getting sick or being involved in an accident and ending up at the hospital. We never plan for this type of thing to happen and certainly don't wish for it, but in reality, it can and does happen. The degree of unpleasantness only increases when you don't understand the doctor or you can't even describe what's wrong. Here's when you will really appreciate having learned some conversational phrases before you move.

How about the possibility that your local school calls you with what you guess is an urgent message about your child, but you can't understand what they're saying? Or that man at your front door you refused to let enter your home who may in fact have been a meter reader with a legal right of entry? Or the morning you can't drive out of your garage due the enormous trench outside your front door, which was clearly announced by notifications you threw away because you couldn't understand them?

When my car broke down on the highway in France, it was raining, cold and storming. In times of slight panic, it's not the most convenient occasion to start learning new vocabulary. I called for roadside assistance, but the friendly operator didn't understand much English. Then came the mechanic with the tow truck, asking me more questions, not speaking one word of English. If you're standing on the side of the motorway in the rain and all you want is to get home and fast, I guarantee you'll dive into the language books after that.

Homonyms (words that sound alike but have different meanings) can be troublesome when learning and using a new language. An American expat shared a story that demonstrates the difficulty regarding words that sound alike: He had ordered in Spanish at a restaurant in Madrid, clearly pronouncing the word, *'caballo'*. The waiter, looking irritated, replied, "Sir, we don't serve horse here." The American thought he was saying *'cebolla'*, which means onion.

As these examples demonstrate, expats need to seriously consider taking the time to learn the local language! This should not only be thought about in the context of problem-solving, but more positively, in the context of opportunity, and increasing knowledge. We're never too old to learn.

Cultural differences and awareness of them is my favourite topic to cover in workshops because it's so fascinating to see people realize how deeply culturally conditioned they are when confronted with diversity.

Are you trying to land a job? Then, showing your willingness to learn the local lingo will also improve your chances of finding suitable work as you are more attractive to potential employers. It starts by adding this skill to your CV, even if only a beginner's level. Employers notice it immediately and I'm convinced it results in an increased number of job interviews. On top of that, it's so much more fun if you can switch away from English during an interview.

Meeting new people while living abroad, be it during social events, at work, or in your neighbourhood, is so much easier and fun when you can hold a conversation with them. You feel integrated when others start talking to you and you are able to understand and answer.

In many places, expats can survive extremely well without any knowledge of the local language. However, if you want to get the most out of your journey abroad, and actually experience and discover things, instead of merely "surviving", then your effort spent gaining a little knowledge of the language will be well worth it.

Where Do They Speak English?

Holiday destinations attracting tourists are often easier because the economy thrives on English-speaking visitors; therefore, most locals will speak English. For other places, it varies, of course. For example, in Scandinavia, and the more northern European destinations, English has been extensively taught in schools for many generations and most locals can speak at least some English. In Western Europe, in countries as France, Spain, Italy, and Portugal, in non-tourist areas, it may be difficult to find anyone who knows more than, "Good Morning" or "Thank You". This also applies in the South-East countries, such as Greece.

In most countries in North and Central Africa, French is still the most widely spoken language besides the local one, while English is largely unknown in many areas.

Moving to South-East Asia and China, the legacy of old colonialism, imperialism, and the more recent phenomenon of tourism means that English is more widely understood but again, mostly used by professional or commercial people.

The main point to remember is that in very large parts of the world, and especially outside of major centers, English is not going to help you much.

No Obligation

Nobody will force you to learn a new language, and as I mentioned before, you will, like countless others, be able to survive abroad without the extra effort. In many situations, it's not a big problem. Going into a local bakery to buy a bread can easily be accomplished through hand gestures and plenty of smiles. You'll often generate friendly and helpful responses from the locals by playing 'the helpless foreigner' and using universally-understood behaviours.

Unfortunately, funny gestures become less appealing and useful when dealing with official institutes. Trying to get your internet, electricity, and other utilities connected in some countries, for example, often comes with much less sympathy, especially over the phone. During a call, you can forget using that smile, and if you want to make some a good impression when dealing with tired and overworked call center employees, your first question should be something other than, "Do you speak English?"

Tips for Learning a New Language

The below tips can help immensely when you're learning a new language. I have practical experience with all of them myself, and find they are helpful for my students around the world as well.

Take, for instance, the below suggestion of watching TV in a new language. Even if you don't understand it yet, your subconscious is picking up a lot more than you think, and it's an easy and fun way to begin learning right away.

Try out these tips and then find ways to challenge yourself every day.

❖ **Watch the local TV:** Try to make the effort to watch or listen to one hour of local TV every day, such as the news, documentaries, TV series, or cartoons.

❖ **Read the local newspaper:** Try reading at least 1-2 pages of it per day, using Google's dictionary.

❖ **Venture out to local establishments:** Get out and discover bars, shops, and restaurants, so you can practice speaking and listening.

❖ **Learn a few new words everyday:** Don't worry about grammar just yet; make your first goal to learn the 100 most common words. Use them or write them down. The more words you know, the more sentences you will be able to form. Ask a local to record key language words and phrases, which you can play over and over as practice.

❖ **Learn a language is with tandem or exchange partner**. You can learn a new language and teach your own language at the same time with another person. Usually through Skype. It works very well to actually learn how to speak and pronounce sentences instead of merely knowing how to write it.

❖ **Immerse yourself in the language**: Aim for a certain amount of daily exposure to the language, via TV, internet, or by getting out and mixing with the locals, face-to- face.

❖ **Learn to count in the new language.** Start by counting from one to ten, because it is usually the easiest thing to memorize at first.

❖ **Learn a few basic greeting words and short phrases:** Hello, good morning, how are you? I speak

English. This gives you a great way to introduce yourself to the locals.

❖ **Watch a movie:** Once you have some basics down, you are ready to watch an entire movie. Pick one you know, but now watch it in the new language, or at least subtitled.

❖ **Listen to music:** Find songs you like and listen to them in the local language over and over again until you start understanding some of the words.

❖ **Talk to children or older people:** They are the ones who tend to have more time and hopefully patience, so you can practice talking to them at a level that shouldn't be too complicated.

❖ **Reading:** Whether it's a magazine or a book, even if you only look at the images and headers, you will keep picking up new vocabulary. Think about topics that interest you to make it pleasant. Comic books, recipe books, anime, or joke books.

❖ **Etymology:** Learning the history of the language can help you better understand it.

❖ **Learn to pronounce the alphabet:** This will help you in your reading and pronunciation, but also in memorizing the words you are learning.

❖ **Learn a few basic greeting words and short phrases:** For example: *Hello, Good morning, Goodbye, How are you? I speak English and a little (fill in the new language)*. This gives you a great way to introduce yourself to the locals, who will appreciate your effort.

❖ **Post-its:** Write down words and stick them everywhere in your house. This helps to activate your subconscious, adding visual association, which helps you to learn faster.

❖ **Use a language App:** Many apps are available to download to your phone so you can practice anytime, anywhere.

❖ **Don't be afraid to make mistakes.** Accept that you will make mistakes and your accent will sound different and funny. Remember you are making the effort to learn and that is very much appreciated by the locals. To learn a language, you must practice. Practice takes time, so be patient.

❖ **Join a language group or exchange languages online:** Every expat group or forum has information about languages, such as where you can find classes in your city. You can also easily find people to exchange languages with. For example, on Internations.com, there are many requests as along the lines of, "I want to learn Spanish and I'll teach you French in exchange," This is absolutely free of charge and a good method if you have the time and a good internet connection to meet with your language exchange partner regularly.

❖ **Get a teacher.** Receiving lessons tailored to your level and speed can be invaluable. You can choose a face-to-face or online session, which saves time and travel. My students range in age and are located all over the world in various time zones. Customized sessions based on your interest, goal, and level can increase progress rapidly and in a pleasant manner.

You've Got Talent

It's true that not everyone has the same ability when it comes to learning a language. Some seem to be naturally gifted, finding pleasure in learning new vocabulary in record time. It is also true that age can play a part - children and younger adults usually find it easier to become proficient in another language than older adults. Raising your children bilingually has so many benefits, it should definitely be every parent's priority. Benefits of being bilingual have been studied repeatedly and in most cases, the outcomes suggest that being bilingual improves the brain's executive function, which is a command system in the brain that directs the attention processes that we use to solve problems, plan, and perform other mental tasks. Also, bilingual kids show cognitive flexibility; that is, they are better at focusing attention on relevant information and ignoring unnecessary distractions. Another benefit is the understanding of math concepts and solving word problems easily, because their brains are active and flexible.

Become One of the Locals

Whether you are bilingual or not, there is rarely an excuse for not even trying to learn the local language, yet the choice is ultimately up to you.

The objective of learning a few basic phrases and words is to arrive in your new home with the ability to understand a few things that may be said to you. Once you arrive, you can continue and expand your level.

If you put in the effort, you will be rewarded by feeling a little more like a 'local' and being able to enjoy your new life, country, and culture a little more. Recognizing words, growing your familiarity, and making short conversation helps you become more integrated and feel more "at home."

Speaking the local language will make you feel more comfortable when out-and-about on a daily basis. It also boosts your confidence remarkably the moment the local people start conversing with you in their own language. That achievement is such a triumph, because just like you physically crossed the border when you moved, this a special kind of moving from being *foreigner* to a *local*.

As a final thought, remember that most people, no matter where you go, are proud of their culture and heritage—at least, to an extent. In some places, refusing to make a serious effort to learn the language may be seen as an insult to them and their culture. There's a different degree of acceptance between a two-week holidaymaker with a funny accent, compared to the individuals that actually move to their country for a longer time.

Of all the hints and tips in this book, the suggestion to learn and use the local language is perhaps the most important. This one thing alone can make all the difference between a pleasant expat experience or one described as a rough and bumpy road. Make the effort and enjoy yourself in the process!

KEY TAKEAWAYS:

→ Taking the time to learn the local language is the most common advice from experienced expats.

→ Whenever possible, start learning the language *before* you leave home.

→ Having a basic grasp of the local language will make your adjustment easier. You will be able to make local friends without relying on fellow expats.

→ Get over your embarrassment and accept you're occasionally going to make a fool of yourself! Just keep smiling!

Chapter 8
Smooth Integration or Culture Shock

> *"You have to taste a culture
> to understand it. "*
> **- Deborah Cater**

When in India…

"*Namasté*," I said when I arrived in India, and naturally raised my arm and reached out my hand, as shaking hands is my custom and polite way of greeting. Yet, my hand was left hanging and I stood there looking silly and feeling awkward. My first cultural lesson came within the hour I had landed. I immediately placed my hands together and proceeding to greet people while keeping my hands nicely on my side.

When in France…

In France, people who know each other quite well, are accustomed to kissing each other on the cheeks in greeting. I knew about this custom and felt very comfortable and confident applying it. Soon, after making some new friends, the moment came where I said, "*Salut,*" and moved my cheek for the friendly greeting. When I was then ready to pull back after one kiss, I saw the other cheek coming for a second, and when I pulled back again, a third and a fourth. At first, I thought it might some sort of special occasion to kiss to many times, but no, the fact is that the common greeting consists of four kisses. And to make it nicely complicated, this is not true of the entire country; there are some areas in the north where they are happy with one kiss, while other areas are used to two or three kisses.

The main thing I took away from this and similar experiences is to observe local customs upon your arrival in any country and watch people greet each other before you attempt it yourself..

One of the things we all have to deal with as expats when we first move to a new place is that sense of unfamiliarity, that awareness of having left our comfort zones. During those first few months after relocating, we get that feeling that we're a "fish out of water"; when we walk down the street, walk into a mall, or drive around the city, we don't recognize anything. This feeling often makes people long for where they came from, and long for familiar sounds, places, food, or faces. This feeling lasts longer for some than others. Finding ways to cope and settle in are important to make the new place feel familiar sooner.

The world is becoming a smaller place every day. The internet makes it so that we're only ever a click away from the other side of the world. In fact, every day, whether I am teaching or holding meetings, I am talking to other people from at least one other continent. Communicating online is wonderful and part of a daily lifestyle for many of us.
Similarly, workplaces become more diverse and more companies do business globally, working with multiple cultures.

Because of this expansion in global reach, the opportunities for cultural misunderstandings are also expanding. Not everyone can be an expert in every culture.

And even outside the corporate world, we are increasingly confronted with various cultures in our daily lives. At school, classrooms are filled with students from all parts of the world. Exchange programs are no longer an exception, with international studies being highly attractive nowadays.

> *"Maybe the funniest part is that here people usually don't save food for more than one day, whereas in Mexico you can keep your favourite dish in the fridge for days because it would be a shame to let something so tasty go to waste. I always get the weirdest looks when I ask: 'Are you really gonna throw that away?? It's still gonna be good tomorrow!'"*
> **- Yasbenia from Mexico**

Let's Talk About Culture

While walking around in any city, you will find a mix of foreigners and locals. Just look around in your own surroundings, your neighbourhood, or even your family, and most probably you don't have to think too long to find someone from another culture.

We live in very interesting times. With social media sites like Facebook, we're only one *like* away from the other side of the world. One click or one call is all it takes to communicate with another culture. Psychology and the study of people has always interested me, but my interest in the subject of cultures has grown with my journeys abroad. Through teaching courses at the university as well as online, I'm fortunate to get to study cultural topics in greater depth.

Without diving into detailed theory, I will provide some typical examples that relate to the most well-known cultural dimensions, which is a framework that distinguishes different cultures.

One of these focusses on how some cultures emphasize individual over group behavior. For example, in Latin-America and Asia the group and the family are far more important than the individual. Western Europe on the other hand, is more focused on the individual and therefore parents are proud when children achieve things on their own, and are independent or I-oriented. The following case explains this:

After studying in the Netherlands for six years, Manuel from Bolivia returns to Cochabamba. His family gathers for a big welcome home dinner where Manuel is very proud to share his experiences abroad: learning Dutch, working nights to pay for his tuition, studying on his own, and cooking for himself!

But his pride is diminished when his aunt responds by saying, "What? Cooked for yourself? Studied on your own? Did you not have any friends? What is wrong with you? Why did you have to work? We could have helped you. We are your family!"

The cultural dimension of time is another distinguishing factor between cultures and attitudes regarding time can differ in quite significant ways. Being late for an appointment is the accepted norm in most Mediterranean countries as well as many countries in Asia. Such habits, though, would torment people in the punctuality-conscious USA, England, Switzerland, etc., where people are very schedule-oriented. Their lives revolve around checking the clock. Time is money, after all. Take for example some countries in Africa and Latin-America: if something starts at 10 AM, you start getting ready at 10 AM. And It works out because everyone involved knows nobody will be there *at* 10 AM.

To this, people in America would say, *"You are running late!"* But people in Africa respond: *"We are not in a rush. We do not live by the clock. We are more casual. It's fine."* For some countries, the words for *"on time"* refer to expected delays of less than one minute, while in many other countries, up to fifteen minutes leeway is still considered *"on-time".*

Speaking your mind is another differing virtue in cultures where answering with a "yes" or a "no" are equally well accepted as part of open and honest communication. However, in cultures where the group and the family matter above all, and where keeping harmony is a virtue, saying "no" is perceived as such a confrontational phrase that people often soften it with a kind "yes".

This means that if you made an agreement and clearly heard a *"yes"*, the meaning behind that "yes" can vary from an "I'm being polite and preserve harmony-yes," to a direct, "I'll do it-yes."

Funny Foreigners

The landscape of cultures is nothing new, but when it comes to communicating with other cultures, people very often encounter complications or embarrassing misunderstandings.

Thankfully, cultural confusions can also be very funny sometimes, and great for dinner conversations years later.

Unusual foods are a typical example that lead to the astonishment of many expats. Common American foods that people in other cultures find unusual include corn on the cob (in some countries, it is solely considered food for animals), popcorn, marshmallows, and crawfish. On the other hand, foods that could concern some Americans going to other countries include shark fin soup in Hong Kong, dog meat in South Korea, and sheep's eyeballs in Saudi Arabia. Or how about some parts of Mexico where chicken soup contains chicken's feet?

Gift-giving etiquette is another example of a challenging cultural difference. During my time in France, I was invited to a dinner where I tried my best to make a good impression as a foreigner, arriving with a bottle of wine for the host. But the French place high importance on their wine selection, and the hosts usually have something else in mind. One alternative would be to bring a high-quality liqueur instead, or to be very safe, bring quality chocolates or flowers. But even then, remember to give an odd number of flowers, but never the number 13, which means bad luck. It's perhaps wisest to ask the florist which type of flowers to give, because chrysanthemums are used for funerals in France, white flowers mean death in the Netherlands, dahlias are best avoided in Spain, and red roses are considered only appropriate for lovers. Easy, right?

Office customs can differ greatly as well. The lunch period in most US companies varies from 30 minutes to an hour, and break times are usually one fifteen-minute period in the morning, and one in the afternoon. They should be kept to the time specified, because Americans are time and productivity conscious and "time is money". Meanwhile, most Europeans have a 1-1.5-hour lunch break, and full twenty-minute-long breaks during the morning and afternoon in addition to some start-up and wrap-up time. That said, while working in Germany, my lunch break was a strict forty-five-minutes and was not flexible. Nevertheless, a 40-hour workweek can in reality mean something quite different depending where you are.

Okay, maybe not at first. But a little research goes a long way toward avoiding offense. Sometimes people find out too late that certain things they may have said or done weren't received in the way they intended. For example, making eye contact is appropriate and often quite important for many Europeans and Americans. Not making direct eye contact can be considered rude, indifferent, or even weak. Yet, in some Asian nations, prolonged eye contact will make a local uncomfortable, so don't be offended if you're in a business conversation with someone who won't look you straight in the eye. Also, when you're toasting with friends in a German, French, or Dutch café, your eyes better meet theirs when you touch glasses. If not, it means you'll suffer seven years of bad sex. Perhaps the best advice is never to gaze too long, observe the behaviour of your host, and follow it.

Another common tradition is taking off your shoes when arriving at the door of your host. In the UK, they might find you uncivilized, but failure to remove your shoes in Asia or Hawaii is a sign of disrespect. Leaving them outside will not only keep the dirt out of the room but also signify leaving the outside world behind. Usually, you'll see other shoes standing in a row at the door, which is a great sign to start undoing yours.

Sometimes, especially in countries with strong religious or cultural taboos, it may be easy to accidentally cause offence or upset someone with a blunt remark or action. For example, in Muslim countries, it is important to remember that Muslims do not eat pork or drink alcohol. They also engage in an annual practice of Ramadan, when they fast during daylight hours for an entire month. While some Muslims might not mind, it might be insensitive to eat in front of Muslim friends or co-workers throughout this time.

Raising Cultural Sensitivity

For each culture comes a set of rules and etiquette-based questions, such as: How do I greet them? How shall I call their names? What shall I wear to dinner? Will they understand my English? Preparing yourself with research will help you find most answers. Cross-cultural training can also help tremendously in your preparation and understanding of a new culture.

Think about the circle of people close to you. How easy, or difficult, it is to get along with them. When was the last time you had an argument with a loved one? It happens to all of us. Maybe you're bickering about being late for dinner, or it might be a bigger issue, such as not approving of your son-in-law. Now think about neighbours, from a similar culture, who might be fighting for years over a tree that hangs in both the yards.

Now, in today's world, where mixed marriages are common, cross-cultural businesses are frequent, and people moving abroad are no longer exceptions, we can't avoid interacting more and more with other cultures. While some people struggle to get along with their own family, from their own culture, it takes effort and flexibility to understand one another. That's the energy needed to sympathize with a new culture and keep miscommunication to a minimum.

Feeling Welcome in Your New "Home"

Most expats unintentionally commit some cultural taboo when they first arrive in a different country, even those countries which appear very similar to their own. Take France and Belgium, two countries right next to each other. That bottle of wine I previously mentioned wouldn't be such a great gift to bring to a dinner party in France, would be quite welcome at a Belgian dinner party. Expats arriving in China might not know about the taboo of holding their chopsticks in the wrong direction, holding them incorrectly in their efforts to just get the food in their mouth without dropping any.

Regardless of how silly or serious the situation, dealing with a completely unfamiliar culture is one of the more challenging aspects when you move for the first time. That's why your preparation and familiarization beforehand will help you adapt to the cultural climate more easily.

Upon arrival, everything can feel new, surprising, and sometimes scary at the same time. Here are some fundamentals to bear in mind:

- Remember it will be frustrating at times when you've had yet another misunderstanding over some cultural custom. Try to think of these missteps as learning experiences.

103

- Occasionally you might need to take a few steps back in order to move forward and become part of the local environment.
- Most locals won't mind if you make a faux pas and are appreciative of you making the effort to learn.
- Remember to be patient when learning and embracing the new culture.
- If you have a partner and kids, make sure everyone settles in well and don't let your own fears influence or magnify theirs. Usually, kids settle in very quickly, especially when they go to school and make new friends.
- Don't forget the cultural discomfort is only temporary and will fade away as you integrate.

Tips and tricks to deal with culture shock:

Living and studying abroad is an exciting and enriching opportunity. Nevertheless, the ways in which you view the world compared to the views,   beliefs,   and customs of people of other cultures may be greatly different. Culture shock refers to the stress and disorientation people experience when experiencing a culture other than their own.

Symptoms of culture shock vary in terms of severity and length depending on the individual and may include the following: discomfort, irritability, homesickness, hostility toward the host culture, frustration, sleeplessness, and other physical expressions of stress.

Some people have a harder time settling in than others. The below practical tips may help you cope with embracing the new while not forcing you to abruptly abandon the old and familiar:

- Arrange for trips back home to see your loved ones and give your spiritual batteries a re-charge.
- Keep in touch with friends and family on a regular basis. Use Skype or Facetime; they're free and easy.
- Journal. Write down your experiences and how you are feeling.
- Exercise! Go out and explore, get plenty of fresh air, and keep your body and mind active. Make it a daily habit and create a routine. Exercise also releases endorphins into your body which can help you feel more positive and cheerful.
- Write a list of all the things that weren't or aren't going so well in your home country. When you feel a sudden urge to return home, read your list and you will remember that home is not always perfect either.
- Take some time to relax! Join social clubs or expat meeting groups, where you can meet people who have gone through what you are going through. Find hobbies that you enjoyed in your home country. Book a massage or spa treatment, treat yourself to a gift, catch up on sleep, spend more (or less) time with your family. Choose any activity that will help to relieve some of that stress you're feeling.
- Learn the local language. Join a language class or find an exchange partner amongst the locals; this will allow you to meet a local and teach them your language in return for them teaching you theirs.
- Don't make any rash decisions. Take the time to absorb and get used to your new circum-

stances. You don't book a return flight when you move abroad for a reason.

- Create routines; they add predictability and help stabilize emotions. Start by identifying a place in your new neighbourhood that you can visit frequently, whether it's a library, a restaurant, a gym, or a mall. Make a routine to go there once or twice per week. Building that habit will be your short-term goal and will become a routine. Once you have routines in place, you will notice the familiarity helps you start to feel more at home.
- Keep in mind that the first year is always the hardest, and you definitely are not alone. Even if you feel like you'll never adjust, one day in the future, you will look back and cherish that experience too.

Most importantly, have fun and make your new culture part of your life and part of who you are. Get out there, take a walk by yourself, observe, and explore a new part of town. Discover a new store on a new street. Read a book on the terrace of an outdoor cafe, or just sit back and watch people walk by. Write everything in your journal so you can read it again in six months or ten years.

Though a culture shock can be painful, overcoming it provides you with a sense of fulfillment and is a step up the ladder of your personal growth. It is definitely a mind-stretching process that will offer you a broader mindset and wider tolerance for others and their way of life.

Returning Home: Reverse Culture Shock

Reverse culture shock is the term used for the experience people may encounter when returning to a place that they expect to feel like home but actually no longer is. It is a surprising situation that's often underestimated by both expats returning and their family and connections who never left home.

While the aim of this book is to prepare you for your departure, I want to briefly detour to bring your attention to the fact that one day, you may return to your native country and experience this challenge.

For some, return comes after six months, and life pretty much just picks up as before you left. For others, the return can be five or fifteen or even more years after they've left. Some may have stayed in only one country, while others have lived in a series of locations abroad, and spent more time adapting to new norms and values. Returning after several years can cause an initial euphoria when spending unlimited time with your loved ones again, because you're not just visiting as a holiday. But that phase eventually wears off, and that's when you might find yourself feeling out of place in your own culture.

Expats returning home can expect some of the following re-entry challenges:

- Boredom
- Feeling that no one wants to listen
- Feeling people don't understand you
- Reverse homesickness
- Discovering relationships you thought remained, have now changed
- People thinking you've changed too much—or not at all

- Feelings of alienation
- Inability to apply new knowledge and skills
- Feeling stuck

How can you combat this reverse shock? As with its counterpart, you may want to try the following:

- Share your experiences with others, even if you feel like no one wants to listen, there will be someone who supports you and is open to hearing you.
- Keep in touch with friends or contacts you made abroad, and share stories with them.
- Keep your international mindset and don't give up your interests to explore. Remain flexible and meet new people, just like you did abroad. People have changed, including yourself, so you might need to look for a fresh circle of people to be around.
- Seek out training or a coach to guide you through the phases of re-entry. This will help you learn about the changes that have happened while you were gone. Basically, you'll need patience and even more of an open mind than before. If you remember to expect the unexpected when you return, just like when you moved away, things will fall into place.

KEY TAKEAWAYS:

→ Understand the dos and don'ts of the new culture beforehand and keep an open mind.

→ Cultural misunderstandings are common during the first months; appreciate the humour of them.

→ Be patient and build a new routine help combat culture shock.

→ Upon returning to your home country, you'll discover life continued while you were gone. Be ready for changes.

Chapter 9
Upon arrival: I'm here, now what?

> "I can't think of anything that excites a greater sense of childlike wonder than to be in a country where you are ignorant of almost everything. Suddenly you are five years old again. You can't read anything, you have only the most rudimentary sense of how things work, you can't even reliably cross a street without endangering your life. Your whole existence becomes a series of interesting guesses."
>
> **– Bill Bryson**

You've finally arrived in your new territory! Months of planning, preparation, and anticipation have led to this day. You've said goodbye to everyone at home and now you are off the plane and about to embark on your new life abroad. If you've done your homework and prepared well ahead of time, you have sorted most of the basics: finances, a job, accommodation, some cultural knowledge, and perhaps a new language—all key matters we discussed previously, which you can prepare ahead of time to make you feel so much more relaxed upon arrival.

Still, certain things are just impossible to prepare for ahead of time or at a distance, such as registering in the local municipality or connecting all the utilities in your new home. Let's run through some crucial ones to help you get started on the right foot. You'll find the short version in a checklist in part two of the book.

> *"Thanks to my preparation and the fact I was holding a work contract, I didn't face big issues upon arrival. The administrations went well and pretty quickly. But still, I couldn't open a bank account or subscribe to health insurance since I had no address in the Netherlands. It is only when I settled in my own apartment that I could sort these matters out. Actually, the most annoying matter clearly was the health insurance. First, I wasn't quite sure I needed one and second, the insurance offer is pretty extended, unnecessarily complex, and never described in a language other than Dutch... Not to mention the ridiculous price of such insurance or the absence of major price difference among the supposed competitors. I just ended-up picking the cheapest one, but still feel this whole system is wrong."*
> **– Laurent from France.**

What to do upon arrival:

- Register your address with the local authorities when you move in. This is usually located in the city hall, where you can receive your I.D. card. You may also need to get a residence permit.
- Register with your local embassy or consulate (if possible). This will help the consulate keep in touch with you if you have any problems
- Arrange for a local bank account

- Arrange for local health insurance (mandatory)
- Check local traffic regulations: is your driver's license permitted or are you able to exchange your license? Perhaps you will need to take an exam and test again to receive a new valid license to drive locally.
- Get connected: arrange internet, phone, TV, and utilities (gas, electricity, water)
- Register with a local doctor and dentist (before you get sick)
- Register with the local municipality (mandatory)
- Collect or arrange a residence permit and/or work permit
- Find or move into your accommodations
- Investigate school/childcare options
- Make an emergency notebook. It may seem like common sense, but when you first arrive, your head is usually all over the place and this can be forgotten. Maybe this seems unnecessary to you and hopefully you'll never need it. Items to include are emergency telephone numbers in your new country. Contact numbers of the ambulance, hospital, doctor, dentist, health insurance, and fire department. If you drive, make sure you know the number in case of an accident on the road, as well as the one for car insurance.

Last but certainly not least: your own number! You'll need it often during registrations, but also to inform your family. We tend to have our previous phone number in our head so it's often good to have your new number written down somewhere.

- Always keep some extra cash, separate in case of emergencies. Not only for an illness or an accident, but also for initial registrations in certain instances. For more info, see the chapter on finances
- Walk, explore and discover. Whilst you are keeping yourself busy with all the registrations and other appointments, it's equally important to become acquainted with your neighbourhood. Find out if there are different paths to your home, where the closest bus stop or train station is. The best way to explore a new city is on foot, and if you can, by running. Personally, I love running and have saved myself a lot of time by taking a few early-morning jogs each time I move to a new place. You can set a whole day aside to have a wander - a day when it's okay to get lost and have your own personal adventure.
- Stay in touch - remember to give your family and friends your address abroad

"As I prepared my first meal in a new city, I opted for the safe and familiar option of home-cooked pasta, purchased from the local supermarket. I settled into my stride in the kitchen, water on boil and looking forward to some comfort food, but as I opened the bag, out tumbled countless dead bugs. My sense of security and excitement evaporated like the boiling water, leaving a feeling of dread and the question of "where have I come?"
– Natasha from the UK

The first weeks in a new country always make me feel excited and awkward at the same time. Stepping out of my new front door, walking down a new street, trying to remember certain houses or street signs so I can recognize my way back to my new home. Upon finding the new supermarket in town, I spend at least one hour inside, only to explore, to stare at the groceries as if I've never seen an apple before in my life. Finally arriving at the cash register, I only have one bottle of coke to pay for, because this is merely a discovery trip, and I'll return later for my real groceries. Then I continue my walk and observe buildings, watch cars passing by, and notice differences with other countries. I carefully look at people walking by, putting a tentative smile on my face while trying to notice if they greet or smile back at me or perhaps notice I'm new. As if I have a sign on my forehead revealing, "I'm the newbie in town."

Those first days abroad are fascinating and I truly enjoy the newness in everything and everyone. It's an exhilarating experience, full of curiosity and eagerness to explore unfamiliar terrains. At the same time, it may also involve a sense of feeling a little lost in the world.

Cruising Through the Stages of Adjustment

Expats almost always go through a period of adjustment when settling in a new country. This period, or cycle of adjustment, can be divided into four distinct stages: honeymoon, frustration, integration, and home phase. During this time, the awareness and attitudes toward cultural differences change and evolve. While this sequence is very commonly used, every expat's experience is individual and you may not go through all the feelings and reactions described here.

115

- The Honeymoon Phase:
  - Lasts one or two weeks
  - Full of curiosity and interest
  - Attitude toward new surroundings is highly positive
  - Your move seems like the greatest decision you ever made
  - Feelings of excitement and fascination
  - Everything is exotic and quaint
  - You overlook minor problems such as the absence of central heating
  - You become captivated by the language, people, and food
  - You may feel like a tourist

> *"Everything in the beginning is like, wow! Everything is efficient. I see beautiful infrastructure, gorgeous flowers everywhere, and nice people. I love it here."*
> **– African expat arriving in The Netherlands.**

- The Frustration Phase:
  - Can last for the first few months
  - Wider exposure to country and culture
  - Irritations about transportations or unfamiliar foods
  - Enthusiasm is tempered with frustration
  - The fatigue of not understanding gestures, signs, and language creeps in
  - Miscommunications are frequent
  - Feelings of homesickness, loneliness, and anxiety can happen

- o Nothing is routine
- o Limited language ability undermines confidence
- o Differences between your home and the new culture become more apparent
- o This is the most difficult stage

"The food doesn't taste good. I miss a good home-cooking. The sun is not warm here in the winter. The friends I make here are superficial and not as real as my friends back home. I feel so alone."
– Dutch expat in Spain.

- The Integration Phase:
  - o Usually happens within 6 to 12 months.
  - o Routines begin to develop
  - o Things start to feel normal
  - o You are somewhat more self-reliant and more self-confident
  - o You feel more familiar and comfortable with the culture and language
  - o Navigation becomes easier
  - o You try new food and make adjustments in behaviour to adapt to the long lines or long waits for public transportation. You feel positive and more relaxed

"I've been invited for dinner at my friends' house and after that we all go out to some really cool places around town. The area is nice, there is plenty to do around here."
– Italian expat in Belgium

- The Home or Acceptance Phase:
  - Happens after other stages have passed
  - You adopt the new culture's style of doing things like taking a midday siesta You're used to being on your own
  - You're able to take care of yourself independently and speak and understand the language
  - You develop friendships with the locals
  - You're more effective at work because you understand the culture better
  - You're referring to it as your "home" now

> *"It's Christmas and I stay here, at 'home'. I won't travel away, this is where I feel good and will have a great time. "*
> **– American expat in Germany**

KEY TAKEAWAYS:

→ Get lost to find your way around your new neighbourhood.

→ Get connected - phone, utilities, TV, internet.

→ Try not to stress; it's normal to feel overwhelmed upon arrival.

→ Stay in touch with the ones back home

Chapter 10
Settling In

I found my way to the supermarket without taking unplanned detours. Finally, I begin to recognize my neighbourhood. When driving to work and back, I carefully listen to my navigation system, directing me through every turn, but when I identify the correct exit on the highway, it puts a smile on my face, knowing where my new home is. My mailbox has my name on it; I memorize my new address and cell phone number and slowly but surely, it is all starting to feel familiar. When a letter arrives with my name and new address on it, even if it's usually some kind of bill, I really start feeling like a local. It's like I always say: "Where ever I live, that's what I call my home."

Living and working in another country, especially in the beginning, involves a series of stressful events, crisscrossed by occasional periods of calm. Once you've completed all the essentials upon arrival, you begin to realize the myriad of adjustments you
have to make. From minor, meaningless things to more profound and serious matters, settling in often includes the following:

- learning new ways of doing things
- learning to do things you've never done be-fore
- stopping yourself from doing things you can no longer do
- adjusting to a completely new bunch of peo-ple
- learning to live and work in a location where you speak a foreign language
- getting used to various new and unusual cir-cumstances
- learning to live without all kinds of familiar routines

After living abroad for many years, I can only see the positives and meaningful sides to the entire process of settling in. Looking back to my first move, I remember the stress I felt wasn't so positive, to say the least. Not just the fear of the unknown, but also having to learn everything for the first time, from finding a house to learning the language to various registrations to get-ting to know the people. The process of settling in may feel fantastic on one day, and then anxiety creeps in the next. It's a rollercoaster of emotions on a ride that lasts for a while.

Here is a list of suggestions from actual expat experi-ences from around the world to help you settle in more easily and successfully:

- **Things you can do with other people:**
  o Invite people over to your house
  o Go to a movie, cafe, etc.
  o Participate in a team sport or fitness class
  o Work as a volunteer for a good cause

- o Find a cycle, walking, or running group

- **Things you can do on your own:**
  - o Read books, newspapers, or magazines
  - o Cook a meal
  - o Take a walk outside
  - o Meditate
  - o Go see a movie
  - o Write in your journal
  - o Go to a restaurant or café
  - o Go shopping
  - o Exercise or join a gym
  - o Take a ride by bike, car, or bus
  - o Watch people while sitting in a café or a park
  - o Study a new language

- **Things to remember during difficult moments:**
  - o This too will pass
  - o I came here to experience a challenge
  - o I've been through worse than this
  - o It's natural to feel down from time to time, no matter where I am
  - o It's not just me
  - o Things didn't always go well back home either
  - o I have taken on a lot; I should expect to feel overwhelmed from time to time

Patience Is a Virtue

Settling in can be a stressful challenge; it takes time, effort, and patience, which for some of us is easier than others. Living in Spain, I spent endless hours waiting in line for every bit of paperwork I needed, whether I was registering for my ID, opening a bank account, getting insurance papers, or waiting for the electricity technician or the dentist. Before moving there, I was used to countries in the North West of Europe, such as Belgium or Germany, where administrative tasks are handled quite smoothly, something I came to appreciate immensely. Nevertheless, I'm grateful to have learned the skill of patience.

Nowadays, anywhere I go for an appointment or meeting, I always carry something to read or write with me, to fill up my time efficiently instead of feeling like I'm wasting it. Now, when my appointments start on time, I find it very surprising and sometimes even wish for more time spent waiting.

> *Stress affects everyone at one point or another and is indeed the biggest health problem. But it's always worth it. The frustrations, disappointments and heartaches are made up for by the fascinations, euphorias, and revelations.*
> **—Expat in Papua New Guinea**

You've Got Mail

Once you are registered as a resident in your new country, the initial excitement subsides, and you realize you are not on holiday. Rather, this place will be your home for the coming undefined time. The moment you no longer need your navigation to find your way home is a sign you're starting to settle in.

It's important to adjust as soon as possible and to realize that life should go on as normal, including daily routines and habits. I usually force myself to get out, talk to local strangers, introduce myself, and build relationships as soon as possible.

Your new house is your special place to come home to every day, so it's extremely important to make it as homey as possible so it feels like somewhere you belong. Of course, at first it looks somewhat bare and unfamiliar, and it's up to you to decorate and make it warm and cozy. Put up pictures of family and friends, use furniture that you had in your old house, and add accessories that mean a lot to you.

A journalist once asked me, "What is the ONE thing that you are emotionally attached to and take with you in all of your moves abroad?" Within one second, I answered, "My big, brown teddy bear." I've had it since I was sixteen-years-old. My parents gave it to me and he has never left my bed since, no matter where I lived. Some nights it sits beside my bed, but not further. She took a picture of it to add to her article.

As silly as it sounds, all of us have some item that we feel attached to, whether it's a teddy bear, a blanket, a picture, or a painting, these objects are important to include, to make you feel home, wherever you are. The sooner your place feels like home, the easier settling in will be.

Meet & Greet at the Gym

One of the first things I do with every new country I'm headed to, and even before I actually move, is search for potential gyms. Then, once I arrive, my list in hand, I begin visiting them. Some destinations have many choices and others not, but checking them out keeps me busy and it gives me a goal for the weekends. Usually you receive a trial session at no charge, so for the first weeks, I enjoy the extra bonus and working out for free. These clubs are great to make contacts. For me, it's the perfect opportunity to talk to like-minded sports people, and find common ground to start a conversation: "Have you been a member here for long?

Can you show me the dressing rooms? Is there a hair-dryer here? Do you take any classes here and which ones? Do you know how this treadmill works?"

Apples and Oranges

Another good way to help yourself settle in is to locate the nearest supermarket and determine whether you recognize any products that you are familiar with. Then, you can explore some new items, which might lead to a pleasant discovery—or perhaps a disappointing one when you think you bought a sweet, tasty jam that ends up being a thick, brown, meat sauce.

Many expats like to search for shops where they can buy favourite foods from their home country. It is common for supermarkets in places like Asia and the Middle East to stock a small quantity of specific Western brands. Even if it can cost up to double the price that you would usually pay back home, sometimes the expense will be worth it. If you need your favourite coffee to kickstart your day, and the local coffee looks like coloured water, you probably won't mind paying extra for your favourite brand of caffeine.

It can be comforting to enjoy a product you've been missing while abroad, but settling in also means integrating into the new environment by cooking with local groceries and maybe using a new kind of shampoo or shower gel. You should not be tempted to try to totally recreate the life you had in your home country in your host country, which muddies the concept of settling in abroad in the first place. Relying on what's familiar will really limit the potential rewards, opportunities and self-development you can achieve by experiencing life in a new culture. And if you need a quick pick-me-up once in a while, you can always ask friends or family to send something over for you or bring something along when they visit.

Make the New Country *Your* Country

If you have a hobby or regular activity that you enjoyed while you were back home, try to keep it up while you are away. If you like to workout at a gym regularly, you should find a gym you like where you can frequently exercise. If you like to eat out, you should find a restaurant that you like and try to make it there a couple of times a month. You will soon get to know the staff, or other regulars, making it a familiar place for you to visit if you are ever in need of company. The same goes for bars or coffee houses. They are all excellent places to socialize, if you put in a little effort and are open to meeting new people.

Creating a routine is the best and quickest way to feel at home, and also, as mentioned in the previous chapter, it helps you to integrate smoothly into the new culture.

Settling into a country means making it your own. Continuing with your usual hobbies will keep your mind off the stress that comes with so many changes and give you a sense of relaxation. Many expat destinations have private clubs where you can meet fellow expats while participating in social events and other activities such as tennis, golf, squash, etc. Alternately, if you like to mingle with the locals, you can easily find things to do in your neighbourhood through billboards, announcements on the radio, posters on shop windows, or brochures in your mailbox. You can always ask someone, local or not, to join you, instead of waiting forever to be invited, plus it's more pleasant when you walk in somewhere new and all eyes aren't focused on you alone. Such awkward situations are mostly experienced by singles, but at least it often forces them to talk to strangers and gain new contacts.

They key to settling in and enjoying your new destination is to embrace the new experience and appreciate everything it offers you. Don't focus too much on what you are missing back home but instead, actively choose to cherish your new location, and any hobbies and activities that wouldn't have been available in your home country. Living abroad can be a truly amazing experience; don't let it pass you by as the result of a self-defeating mindset. Reset your expectations and admire the experience.

Starting a new life in a foreign country is the perfect time to reassess your priorities. What do you want to do? Who do you want to be? It's never too late to reinvent yourself!

Be a Tourist in Your Own Town

Take time to enjoy new experiences. While it's important to stay in touch with loved ones back home, nothing should stop you from exploring your new place. Do the touristy things you've always wanted to and make the most of it! Don't be shy—climb the Eiffel Tower, admire the Sydney Opera House, stroll around at the Taj Mahal, and then sample the local cuisine while you're at it.

Venturing out on your own can be a fun and adventurous way to explore your new area. But maybe you prefer to avoid turning circles around the same building because you can't seem to find the right street. In that case, joining tourists on a guided tour could be a great option for you.

Most residents don't take the time to enjoy being a tourist in their own city or country and prefer to cross borders on their holidays. Bus trips or boat tours are a great way to get an overview of the city and its facilities, plus they are especially time-efficient. That said, you have to like them. If you are not particularly fond of tours, you can opt to instead to read promotional brochures by travel companies in your city.

Most cities also have a full city profile online. Their websites inform you about important news, events, facilities, and other data about the city. Reading these can help you feel more settled in your new home.

Be a New You
Don't be afraid to enjoy some "me time" too. Give yourself time to settle in and concentrate on enjoying every second of life in your new surroundings. Maybe you'll find something you always wanted to do, but never found the time to do it back home.

That's the beauty of being an expat and the part I love most about moving to a new country. Nobody knows you yet, and even when you meet new people, they don't know your past or family and friends back home. Basically, you can start from scratch and turn over a new page, a blank one that you can fill in as you wish. This may sound shady or suspicious, but I can give you some examples: when I got divorced from my dear husband of ten years, everybody in our home town knew us very well, especially as we had run a local bar for many years. I moved to Spain while this was still very fresh. No one I met there knew about my divorce and I had no interest in telling anyone either. Why would I make my life more stressful by bringing this topic into conversations? On the contrary, if I had still been living in back home, everyone would've constantly been asking me about it or worse, I probably would've run into my ex almost every day in such small town. I'm sure you understand the relief I felt to be living abroad in such a situation.

This ability to make a fresh start can be connected to many life events—maybe you had surgery, lost weight, or dyed your hair and look different. Nobody can notice there's a difference; in your new surroundings, this is "you" and there's no history to content with. If you decide to dress entirely differently, nobody will think anything of it. You are free to be whomever you want to be!"

> *"Expect to feel embarrassed, foolish, and sometimes inadequate. It's all part of the experience. These trying times are what we eloquently call 'adjustment'. They're difficult, natural, and useful."*
> **–Anonymous expat in Kenya**

Be Positive

Train your brain to create positive energy. You deserve to enjoy your adventure and feel excited as you explore the world. My most important piece of advice, regardless of where you land or your reasons for moving abroad, is to stay positive and motivated at all times. Easier said than done? Perhaps so, but nevertheless, do whatever it takes to keep a smile on your face when times get tough. Make sure you exercise, socialize with new people, read, travel, explore, attend motivational conferences, or find inspirational talks online. Remember that even if you still lived in your home country, problems can occur. Whether you are working or not, find a way to keep your mind and body active. Train your brain to focus on the good, the things you can learn and experience instead of scanning for problems. It takes effort to train your mind, just like it takes effort to work out your body. It's easier to think negatively just like it's easier to lay back on the couch and do nothing. If happiness is what you're after, know that by training your brain, you can reprogram your mind to find happiness.

Be open, trusting, patient, and enjoy the unique experience. Have fun, listen, smile, embrace change and discover more about the world and yourself.

"The hardest time is at the beginning, when you first move into your village. Being alone, as the only foreigner, takes some adjustment. No matter how much you love it, there are some days when you've just had it."
—Expat in Sri Lanka

Additional Tips for Settling In

- **Meet your Neighbours**

  Knowing the people in your new neighbourhood and being close to them is very important when you move abroad. Even before I move in, I like to meet them, or at least find out who they are; a family with children or an elderly couple. I like to know what to expect once I live there. When you actually move in, use an evening or weekend to visit your neighbours and introduce yourself, maybe get to know them. Alternately, you can choose to invite them for a housewarming party, which could either lead to a no-show, depending on the customs of the culture you landed in, or you could become the nicest neighbour of the block! In addition to the social benefits, neighbours are a great resource for asking questions about your new neighbourhood.

- **Perfect your language skills**

  If you don't speak the language, but followed the advice to start learning ahead of time, you can now begin to upgrade your comprehension. If you haven't got a clue of what anybody says or what anything means, it's time to shift gears and put your brain to work using the tips in the previous chapter on languages.

  Once you know the basics, you can make small talk with the locals, at the newspaper stand, the café, the supermarket, or a restaurant.

  Being able to talk to the locals makes you feel more like one of them, which helps with a smoother integration. You'll also often be appreciated by the locals for your efforts. Alternately, or even additionally, you can always to turn to expat groups who speak English or take language courses, which will also help you to get acclimated.

- **Join Groups and Attend Events.**
  Meetup groups gather all over the world, unless you are in a remote area. No matter where you are, you can always join these forums or groups online and find events nearby.

  Also, if you change the location settings on your social networks such as Facebook and Twitter, you will receive invitations to local events and clubs. These events are a great way to meet new people in your area who share your interests. The events will also make you familiar with the different venues across your new town.

  Even if you don't attend such events, like me when I was living in more remote areas, I still enjoyed making connections online on expat blogs or forums where I could always count on finding answers to my questions. Usually I seek out these forums in advance so I can ask about the culture or customs or places to go and not waste time searching upon arrival. Usually you have more time to research this in advance while you are still in your familiar environment instead of searching around in a location where everything and everyone is new.

Expat Online

Thousands of expat sites are available online; all you have to do is type those words in the search bar and add your destination to make your search even more specific. Since websites come and go all the time, I won't give you a long or comprehensive list, which might be outdated by the time you hold this book in your hands, but I would like to mention a handful of well-known sites and forums that have grown over decades, are unlikely to disappear anytime soon, and may be of use in your research.

Internations https://www.internations.org/ The world's largest global expatriate network with nearly three million members, with communities in 390 cities worldwide. It contains a wealth of informative articles as well as meet-up groups, a marketplace, expat events, guides, forums, etc.

Expat.com http://www.expat.com/ This site provides free information and advice to expats and soon-to-be expats, by inviting them to share their experiences.

Expat Forum http://www.expatforum.com/ One of the largest international expatriate communities on the internet. The site is organized into several sections with forums and articles regarding the most popular expat destinations across the globe.

ExpatExchange http://www.expatexchange.com/ A site filled with resources, guides, forums, and even job postings to help anybody looking to settle abroad.

Just Landed https://www.justlanded.com/ A site with an expat community, advertisements, housing, a job portal, and much more.

Expat Careers – https://ExpatCareers.com/ The premier worldwide, all industry expatriate job site.

LinkedIn https://www.linkedin.com/ LinkedIn operates the world's largest professional network on the Internet with more than 500 million members in over 200 countries.

Meetup https://www.meetup.com/about/ This site brings people together in thousands of cities to do more of what they want to do in life. With over 30 million members, people meet, do, explore, teach, and learn the things that help them feel alive.

You can also find forums specific to any region, such as *Irish Expats*, *Living in Indonesia*, *Expats in Amsterdam*, and the list goes on.
Forums are full of advice from people willing to help make your relocation as smooth as possible since they've experienced similar situations.
Very often, you'll make lots of friends along the way! My first choice is always *Internations*, where I always receive the answers to the questions I post–and it's free.
The internet is a wonderful resource, full of helpful articles and advice from people in the know. But do keep in mind that even if Google can be your friend, the internet is also packed with myths, rumours, and absolute nonsense. Take everything you read with a pinch of salt.

Advice for Homesick Expats
Moving abroad, regardless of why you are there, will always be complicated. The experience can be amazing, exciting, unforgettable, and eye-opening, but also filled with challenges. From finding milk in the supermarket to adjusting to a culture where they eat lunch at 3 PM and dinner at 10 PM, moments of doubt and dissatisfaction are not uncommon.

Especially the first time you move abroad, you will undoubtedly experience some acute form of anxiety or emotional distress resulting from feeling disconnected from familiar people and places. In other words—you will be homesick.

133

It's difficult adjusting to a new environment. You feel lonely and miss your familiar routine, your family, friends, and neighbourhood. You long for your kitchen with your food and drinks and being able to find your way around automatically. You wish you could just speak your native language.

Homesickness can arise soon after arrival, or after a few years, and it doesn't usually go away overnight. It takes effort to get through it, and even if it seems impossible at the time, it is doable, and well-worth the effort. Overcoming homesickness will enable you to see everything around you in a new, more positive light. Each individual has his or her own way of overcoming homesick feelings, but one thing is certain for everybody: nothing will change unless you put in some effort.

Here are a few tips that can help you beat the blues of homesickness and see life through rosy glasses a little sooner:

- **Decide that the new place is your home.** Make the decision that from now on, that is your sanctuary. After all, home is where the heart is.

- **Stay in touch with the people you miss back home.** E-mail, Skype, Whatsapp, or Facetime. While staying connected to your loved ones, also find a way get out and then share your experiences abroad with your friends and family back home.

- **Find a somewhere nice to visit frequently.** This can be a gym, a library, a coffee shop, a restaurant, or a bookstore. Alternately, join an activity group or class. At first, you might feel uncomfortable in these places because you're the newbie, but this feeling quickly switches to discomfort with others after you get to know them. Simply keep going, and "fake it till you make it". In no time, there will be another newbie whom you can put at ease as you've passed that stage and feel a lot more comfortable.

- **Go and explore your new surroundings.** Walk around a lot, run, bike, or drive, and take different routes. Get lost a few times and you'll begin to recognize the area better until you finally start to feel at ease.

- **Eat local food.** Taste different things and find food that you enjoy, so you'll know what to order next time. Make the effort and learn to appreciate local traditions.

- **Make a list of places to explore in your new country.** Do some research and make it your project. It could be a list of villages, cities, theaters, or boat trips. **Create a routine.** Establish routines to feel a sense of familiarity. Whether you work or not, find regular habits that are fun and that you look forward to. It could be yoga class at the gym, a Sunday mountain bike ride with a biking group, or meeting friends at the bar on Friday nights. You'll feel like you have a goal, a purpose, and it helps to beat homesickness, almost guaranteed!

- **Exercise!** This is crucial! At home or abroad, exercise is key to feeling not only healthy and in shape physically but also mentally. Make a plan that allows you to get some exercise and fresh air every day. Go for a run, go to the market by bike or just try to walk as much as possible during your lunch break, whichever you prefer, just make an effort to create healthy habits. Your body will be happier, and you will feel better!

- **Take a piece of home with you**. Your favourite pillow, night lamp, vase, or a clock you received from grandma. Take pictures of your family, friends, and pets. If you have a painting that you've always loved, take it with you and hang it on your new walls.

- **Put yourself out there and create a network in your new surroundings.** Socialize with other expats as well as locals. Meeting people and making new friends is essential to avoid feeling isolated.

- **Accept your feelings of homesickness** and remember it is a very common experience among adult expats and even more common among expat children. There is absolutely nothing to be ashamed of. When you become aware of your feelings and even talk about them with others, it will help you overcome them.

- **Remember that it's worth it.** Do not forget that you are in the middle of an amazing opportunity. If you find yourself doubting that, think about all the challenges you faced and overcame. The stories and personal growth that you are offered through this journey are yours and will stay yours forever.

KEY TAKEAWAYS:

→ Get to know your neighbours
→ Learn the local language
→ Join a group, club, or association to meet new people
→ Get active in the local and/or expat community

Chapter 11
Life as an Expat Partner

While most expats move abroad independently and rapidly dive into their new employment, there are still thousands of expats who arrive in a new location looking for something to do, and after the initial excitement of relocation fades, these expats often wonder how to rebuild their lives abroad. This is often the case for retirees or anybody who decided to relocate with no intention or need to be employed. This is also often the case with expat spouses, who have followed their partner abroad.

The experience of moving abroad can be very different for trailing partners and adjusting to the local and cultural traditions often have a stronger effect on their personal. Typically, the working partner has an easier time adjusting to the new culture because of their built-in daily schedule and new work environment which includes colleagues and familiar tasks. Even expat children make friends at school and have their own daily routine that includes playing and homework.

But for the person who's at home, the one without a job title, a bank account, or any plans for the immediate future, settling in is more of a challenge. The trailing spouse is often living in the shadow of their working partner, which can make life difficult and put a lot of strain on the relationship. Aside from the boredom of having nothing to do every day besides cook meals, clean the house and maybe pick up the kids, it's the overall lack of purpose that seems to be the biggest challenge. This doesn't usually settle in during the first few weeks or "the honeymoon phase" as we talked about earlier, but after that gets old, the trailing spouse may begin to miss having a daily schedule, a purpose, a goal in life.

> *"My husband only has a 1 year contract here, but I took the chance (or RISK) to experience a new country. So, I left my job at the end of last year and it's very strange now, how I fill my days. I used to have a nice daily routine but now the routine is GONE. No more schedule…no more regular job, no fixed salary…and well…it feels stressful actually. This is not a holiday for me, I need a job and I want a job routine instead of standing in the kitchen and surfing the internet every day. So hopefully a job will appear… something."*
> **- Erika from Indonesia**

The spouse is the one who needs to redefine their routine, find daily activities to stay busy and build up a new identity. This includes making friends you can call your own, avoiding only meeting people through your spouse. Expat spouses need to make an effort to participate in activities outside of their partner's work and social life.

All these changes place a great deal of pressure on expats and their spouses, which can act like a magnifying glass on a marriage. Former underlying issues and disagreements quickly resurface, and it doesn't take long to find out if your relationship will pass the test.

In my case, the very first time I moved abroad, I was still married. I made sure to apply and secure a job before leaving home. My husband at the time followed my expat dream with the intention to find a job upon arrival. We would then live and stay abroad happily ever after. That dream lasted only six months, shattering when my (now ex) husband took a flight back home. The next time I flew back was to sign the divorce papers in court. After a visit with my family, I quickly returned abroad because I loved my new home, which then became Spain.

Of course, not all relationships can't endure the process of moving abroad. Though it is a time of severe emotional pressure, moving abroad together can help couples to learn how to work as a team.

Tips for Surviving as the Trailing Partner

Despite the initial loss of their professional identity, expat partners often discover there is a new life to be lived outside of work. By exploring what's out there, they learn to make the best of their time abroad. What works for one person may not work for you, but here's a list of suggestions to get you started:

- Acknowledge your blues: Awareness is half the cure. That saying goes for many things in life, and is definitely true in the case of an expat spouse. Some wrestle with maintaining their self-identity, others struggle to feel

141

connected in another culture because they see their stay abroad as temporary. Some experience the loss of professional identity as extremely frustrating because the job opportunities aren't the same abroad, or require the hassle of visa requirements and other obstacles. Understanding the underlying reasons for how you feel and acknowledging them should be your first step toward dealing with expat blues. Take time for some self-reflection by holding up a mirror to your thoughts and feelings.

- Connect with your support network at home and create a new one abroad: it's important to keep in touch with your family and friends back home, but that alone isn't enough. If you live in an area or city with other expats, you can join expat social groups who are going through the same thing as you. Sharing your experiences can help with coping with your blues abroad. You can also join local groups to make friends with area insiders.

- Online support is always there: If you live in a more rural location and lack an in-person expat network, get online. Expat forums and expat blogs exist all over the world and are there to provide a sense of community. You will easily find others in the same shoes as you who are willing to help by sharing their experiences and advice.

- It takes time: Be realistic about how long it takes to feel comfortable in a foreign country. If you moved within your own country, it would take time to adjust as well, so don't take things too seriously for at least 6 months to a year.

- Do something that fulfills you: Filling your days can be difficult in a new country with little social life and no job to go to. Household tasks can fill some hours, but won't provide you with a great feeling of satisfaction and achievement. Besides picking up long lost or new hobbies while abroad, you can also find volunteer jobs. If you have kids, you can participate in a parent-teacher organization. Find fruitful ways to fill your days and they won't feel so long.

- Find your way around: Learn to find your way in your neighbourhood as soon as you can. Walk around, bike, explore. Learn the local transportation system as soon as possible so you're not stuck at home alone while your spouse is working. You may soon be the one explaining directions to your partner.

- Create a schedule: If you're not working, find ways to incorporate structure into your day as though you were. Wake up at a regular time, get dressed, get groceries and clean on fixed days. And make sure you stick to your schedule. Even exercise and other hobbies are part of a good routine. They make your daily life meaningful and structured instead of feeling you are the unlucky one staying home, watching the clock go by while feeling completely unproductive.

- Talk: Keep an open dialogue with your partner. By respecting the fact that you are both facing new challenges, you can create a sense of mutual support. Involve each other in all kinds of decisions. By simply sharing daily experiences, you strengthen the bond between you and contribute to a healthy family life.

- Develop new interests you've always wanted to pursue. How often we want to do something new but lack the time or opportunity. Living in a new country is the perfect time for this. All you have to do is start.

- Do things together: Go out on dates (with or without the children), watch movies or TV, have a nice dinner. It doesn't have to be super fancy. Just make time for yourselves as a couple. It doesn't matter what you do. Just remember to have your own lives too. Understand your spouse's situation: your spouse is adjusting to a new work environment and faces unique pressures on their side, just like you. Even if it seems things are easier for them as they have a job with structured tasks and responsibilities, it takes time to adjust to the new environment, colleagues, and ways of working in the new culture. When arriving home in the evening, your spouse deserves and appreciates some relaxing time and is not always capable of dealing with more challenges coming from you. Find ways to share without piling on. Understanding each other's situation is vital. It takes two to tango. Maybe you can learn from each other, to thrive abroad.

KEY TAKEAWAYS:

→ Feeling blue? Acknowledge it and accept it takes time

→ Create your own schedule, routine, and plan for the future

→ Understand your spouse's situation. They're adjusting too

→ Do something new you've always wanted to do

Chapter 12
25 Top Tips

Over the past several years, I've interviewed expats from all over the world. At the end of each interview I asked the same question: What is your best tip for potential expats?

From the entire pile of interviews, the most common tip that 95% of them shared is: learn the language!

These expats made many more suggestions that I hope you find helpful. Some of them are rather original, some logical, and others are life lessons that you may find yourself relating to. So, sit back, relax and let yourself be inspired by the following statements:

"No matter how difficult your goal seems to be or how scared you are, just push yourself to take the first step and you'll realize how suddenly you feel strong enough to take the next ones."

"I should not have been shy about making mistakes when speaking the local language."

"Try to join more social activities to get more familiar with the local community since the beginning." –Yasbenia from Mexico

"Do your best to learn the language and understand the culture before moving there."

"For those just coming here and settling in, what I can share is the importance of surrounding yourself with people who can lift you up. Life in a new country with new people becomes somehow easier and more enriching when you have friends that you can call your family."
- Lana from the Philippines

"Just be yourself. Be open and see the chances that come along and work for it!
Do or do not. There is no trying."-Nu from China

"Step out of your comfort zone; that is where the magic begins!"- Alessandra from Italy

"Learn Dutch! So many people say they are going to do it or start and then give up but keep on trying, you can do it. Life here is so much better since I speak Dutch. I understand everything around me, letters in the mail, cooking instructions on food, the news, etc. You also really see people differently when they are speaking in their native language. I was really surprised to see a different side of so many people after speaking to them in their own language after only knowing them in English. You will also be invited to things that you otherwise may not have been invited to, say a party or get-together. They really don't want to speak English all night just because you are there. "- Nick from the USA

"Language is STEP ONE! You can't understand people's character if you don't speak it! So, go to the pub! Be with people! Start with, 'Hi, I'm Robert, Je ne parle pas Français.' Tip TWO = Get involved in culture, country, cuisine, and make an ef-

fort to integrate without losing your nationality." –Russel from the UK

"Remember: people are the same everywhere. We all eat, drink, go to church or mosques. We are human beings."-Ab from Egypt

"TIP #1: Bring your preferred items e.g. your laptop, tablet, and items from your expertise or skills. The items that define you. I hold on to my personal stuff and tools that remind me of 'me' and of what I do. It keeps me from stress and unknown things. Such items bring me back to myself.

TIP #2: Don't be afraid to make friends with someone new. Don't isolate but try to connect. Make an effort with anybody, not only locals. Don't close yourself up.

TIP #3: If you can't find a fixed (full-time) job as an expat yet, try to find VOLUNTEER jobs. This way, you can start to meet new people, create new connections, and also get new and valuable experience by being a volunteer in the causes that interest you. "- Erika from Indonesia

"Try to integrate! Do not isolate by being an expat. Go out there! Don't be too hard with yourself and go back home sometimes."-Lidia from Italy

"The best tip I can give is to carefully prepare prior to moving!!! More specifically, I mean to "close the work chapter", get a contract as an employee or an entrepreneur prior to your arrival. Nowadays, technology allows us to browse for job openings or corporate information as well as to apply remotely."-Laurent from France

"Get familiar!!! I mean, BEFORE you move, look up places to see and things to do. Get informed about where you will be living!"-Joyce from Australia

"My number one tip would be to be flexible and patient. You're moving to a place that's not like home–that's why you are moving there, isn't it? So, things won't be the same as you've known in the past. People may not speak the same language, things won't work the same, schedules may be slower, life may seem confusing. My advice would be to relish the differences. Don't get impatient that things aren't the same as you're used to; appreciate that people do things differently. Keep a sense of humour. Write a blog if you're a writer so you can share those differences with the world. And be grateful that you have the opportunity to live somewhere else. Millions of people around the world don't have that opportunity."-Gabriella from the US

"Be open to see people as just humans just as you are. Forget the prejudice about race, sexual preference, lifestyle, or religion. You will find every kind of people here."-Nathalia from Brazile

"Learn the language! Yes, everyone speaks English, but you won't really get to know people until you speak their language, understand their culture and mix in their lives. Expats will be your lifeline, your 'family' here; they understand but make the effort (and it will be more effort in the beginning because they always want to speak English to you) to speak the local language."-Alison from the UK

"My top tip is to get involved with the local community around you. In whatever way you can, be that a knitting club, running club, school helper, inviting the neighbours over–do mix with the locals! "

"Life is what you make of it."
"First, Learn the language and the culture.
Number 2: If you have little ones, the local libraries are a great place to start meeting people especially if they have a Mamas Café once a week!
Number 3: Don't be afraid to mingle with the locals and even at work. People are very friendly and also willing to assist where they can!"- Nadia from S-Africa

"My TIPS: (T) talk to as many people as you can;
(I) inquire as much as is possible,
(P) participate when and where you can, in order to…(S) settle."- Deborah from Canada

"In general, I recommend watching first before you start commenting or talking. Take the time to watch the people around you and how they interact. You can find out what is ok and what isn't, just by watching.
TIP#2: Stop comparing your home country with the host country. There is nothing better or worse, but rather different. Follow the major rule: If you want to be a Roman, do like the Romans do."-Kornelia from Germany

"My biggest tip: Never ever have any expectations for anything abroad. Not about events, or about people. Take it all as it comes and be creative enough to make it work for you or just get an experience. Flexibility comes with the courage to move. After this, all works for you.
Now, most importantly, research before the departure! But don't expect too much, sometimes what we need is the ability to cope with surprises, whatever those might be."- Milena from Bulgaria
"Have friends from different nationalities, that will enrich your life in all ways.

Don't compare yours and your host country.
Open your heart and your mind to learn and experience new traditions, flavors and ideas.
If you are a stay-at-home wife/mum, find a passion to devote your time to, otherwise, you might end up having shopping as your new hobby." - Carmita from Venezuela

Conclusion

Imagine you're ninety-five years old with little life left to live. You look back over your life and wonder what goals you had that you never pursued. Dreams that you really wanted to fulfill before other things interfered. Maybe fears, worries, or others' opinions kept you from doing what you really wanted. People often say, "life got in the way," or "I had no choice," when they feel they were forced to give up on a dream.

That is the thought I had when I was 24 years old. I had dreamed about moving abroad, but I didn't then, and was 100% certain I didn't want to grow old wondering, "What if I had done it? What if I had moved abroad years ago?"

That thought was my drive, my power, my engine that kept me going from the decision to first move, to all the moves that followed. Even to this day, I'm not done moving yet.

Life is an adventure and I'm happy to have created this journey for myself. It's not always easy, but I know I can now grow old with no regrets and no missed dreams, because I've done it.

With this book, I have taken you through the ins and outs of the amazing adventure of journeying abroad, while sharing a mix of my own expat experiences and the experiences of numerous other expats I've interviewed.

After spending many years abroad, I am more aware of the mountain of knowledge it has brought me, and even more so, the strong personal growth one can gain in becoming an expat.

After reading through all the tips, tricks, checklists, and information, I hope you are well equipped for your own journey abroad.

Another great fact is that as an expat, there are typical characteristics that you develop, which can be an asset for the rest of your life and can definitely give you an advantage in your future endeavors, from jobs to relationships. These traits include adventurousness, cultural sensitivity, curiosity, adaptability, flexibility, and open mindedness. Last but not least, you build self-confidence, which is an amazing journey as reflected in my bestseller, *Awaken Your Confidence*.

Living abroad, you are in a rare position to expand your expertise and skills in so many ways, it is hard to sum them up in a list. Everyone is unique and you will grow in your own way, on your own journey.

Whether you were dreaming of a life abroad or already had plans to relocate before reading this book, the decision to actually move is entirely yours. Maybe you discovered you'd rather not leave your home country, or maybe you gained the courage and motivation to plan your journey. Whatever your decision, stay, leave, or return, there's no right or wrong path. Everyone has their own preferences that can be modified any time. Life changes, and so do we.

It's time for you to enjoy, to wander and explore your new world. Be open, trusting, and patient. Living abroad is an exercise in embracing change and discovering more about yourself and the world. Prepare well, have fun, smile, and just GO!

Wishing you all the best on your journey, wherever the road may take you.

PART TWO

Checklists

The following compendium of lists is designed to help you organize and plan your move abroad. While these lists cover many of the most common situations, they are certainly not all-inclusive, nor do they apply to every situation Regardless, I hope you find these lists help you on your journey!

The below section can be viewed as a general overview of all the things you need to keep in mind while preparing for your move abroad.

Prior to moving

❐ BE PREPARED - Moving abroad is not the same as going on holiday. Proper planning and research is key to a successful move.

❐ WHY? - What is the real reason you're moving? Whether to start a new career, to study, to earn more money, to gain self-confidence, to find a better climate or to retire. Knowing your reason will help you narrow your research and save time.

❐ DESTINATION - Your new location is a key factor. Just like buying a car, take time to research and evaluate several options. Things to consider include climate, religion, crime rate, housing, the economic and political situation, employment options, etc.

❐ BE CERTAIN - Be as sure as you can that the move is right for you. This applies not only to the destination and reason for moving, but also ask yourself if you are the kind of person who can live abroad.

❐ FAMILY - Inform your family and friends of your plans and new address. Be prepared for a rollercoaster of reactions. Stay in touch with the home front after your move.

❐ JOB- If you need to work abroad, ensure you look into the issue of employment beforehand. Start a job hunt well ahead of time while you are still in your familiar and comfortable home town.

☐ DECLUTTER - Start decluttering early, because it always takes longer than you think. Collect all your paperwork in your cabinets, cupboards, desk and elsewhere and begin the organizing task.

☐ LANGUAGE - The number one tip from expats around the world is: learn the language. Speaking or understanding the local language will help you integrate smoothly and create a more positive experience. Starting to learn beforehand is recommended.

☐ PAPERWORK - Usually the least fun, but if you prepare well, it saves you tons of stress abroad. This may include: passport, Visa, birth certificates, medical certificates, educational degrees, and wedding certificates. Make copies of important documents; scan and email them to yourself, just in case of loss.

☐ YOUR HOUSE - Decide if you will sell or rent your current house, or if someone will take care of it while you are gone. What kind of accommodations will you move into abroad? Consider hiring a real estate agent to advise you.

☐ HEALTH - Make sure the country you are moving to has adequate healthcare facilities to support you (and your family). Find out how to register ahead of time, and make sure you are insured appropriately.

❏ YOUR BELONGINGS - Decide between what you really need and what you could store or get rid of.

❏ POST REDIRECTION - Arrange to have your mail redirected to your new address. You won't be able to think of everyone you'll need to inform about your address change and this will prevent you from missing something important.

Who to notify your Change of address:

❏ People, companies, and organizations to inform.
❏ Family and friends staying behind
❏ Colleagues, employer
❏ bank(s)
❏ Loans
❏ Insurances (house, health, vehicle, travel, etc.)
❏ Pensions
❏ Motor vehicle department
❏ Taxation office
❏ Local council
❏ Schools
❏ Dentists
❏ Doctors
❏ Utilities such as water, electricity, gas, internet
❏ Phone
❏ Newspapers or magazines
❏ Online shopping sites
❏ Any other subscriptions and memberships

❏ FINANCES - Do you have savings set aside in case of emergencies? What if you suddenly have to move back? Calculate what everything is going to cost and plan your budget. Make sure you have some money set aside for your transition period. Decide to close or keep your current bank account and find out how to open a new account abroad.

☐ MEET PEOPLE - Make friends, locals or fellow expats. Nothing will help you more than being able to rely on the assistance of your friends when you need it. Don't think that socializing is time wasted; it's what makes a new country feel like home.

☐ REMEMBER YOU WILL GET THROUGH THIS - Moving to a new country is challenging and a high-ranking stressor, even if you plan well. You will experience times when you're physically and emotionally exhausted and you doubt everything. Don't let pessimism wear you down. Remember you are not alone and you can always reach out to expat forums for extra support.

☐ **MAKE THE MOST OF IT!**
No matter how long you are staying abroad, make the most of it. It's an amazing experience, even if some days it doesn't feel like it. Later, looking back, you won't regret anything if you made the most of your time in the new country. Enjoy the new culture, the people, the food, and the surroundings. Join new activities, visit traditional festivities, participate where you can, and most importantly, enjoy your new life!

Research Your Move

☐ Look into guide books, websites, TV programs, etc. about your destination country.

☐ Use a **notebook** or computer to keep track of the information you've gathered as well as items to discuss with your friends and family.

☐ Learn about the country's history, **culture and values**, cuisine, religion, etc.

☐ Find out if you and/or your family need to apply for a **visa**, which is an official endorsement in a passport to authorize your entry into a foreign country.

☐ If you intend to **work** abroad, check if a work permit is required, which allows you to work in a foreign country.

☐ Learn about the **weather** throughout the year and determine how comfortable you will feel.

☐ Evaluate if any **legislation** is likely to affect you, e.g. the right to buy property, taxation, insurance, etc.

☐ Assess your level of conversation in the **local language**. Determine the importance of studying prior to moving in order to live and work abroad.

☐ Join online **expat forums/groups** to meet and chat with expats who already have experience with your chosen destination and can share their own experiences with you.

❏ **Visit** the country before moving (if possible). Remember life as a resident is different than as a tourist.

❏ Note the possible the **time difference** and dates of public holidays.

❏ Consider if you would benefit from a professional **cross-cultural program** or **coach** to help you adjust smoothly. For some, one conversation is enough to gain clarity, for others, they can help in creating a plan for smooth transitions.

❏ **Driver's license** - find out if you need to apply for a new license or are able to convert your current license.

❏ Find out if **electronic devices** such as your phone, TV, lamps, alarm clock, etc. will work in the new country.

❏ Review the **procedure for opening a bank account** in the destination country, paying attention to any paperwork which needs to be completed and/or documents presented.

❏ Ensure appropriate **banking facilities** are available to you abroad.

❏ Assess the **cost of living** abroad. Compare the typical monthly costs (food, rent, travel, leisure etc.) with your current circumstances.

❏ Plan for your **personal safety** by managing the risks associated with moving to and living in a foreign country. Find out the procedure and contact numbers of emergency services.

165

❒ Research how **healthcare** is provided and how the national health system is structured so you know how to use it. Can you easily find and register for healthcare providers (doctor, midwife, hospital, dentist, therapist, etc.) located near your intended address? Ask existing expats for their recommendations and experiences.

Plan Your Move

Create a detailed and realistic plan to help you move while using the following list of items.

Using your notes, you will be able to prioritize your tasks, change them as needed, and then check them off as you complete them:

❒ **Utilities** such as gas, electricity, cable, and so on will need to be informed of your move to terminate contracts.

❒ Get quotes from shipping and **moving companies** if you are moving yourself, without company support.

❒ Make appointments with your **doctor** if vaccinations, medicines, or check-up are necessary.

❒ Make appointments with your **vet** to prepare your pets for the new country.

❒ Schedule time to study your new **language** either by yourself or with a teacher. During conversational sessions, I always include roleplays with practical **day-to-day dialogues**. Adding those to your study will help you immensely upon arrival.

❏ If you are packing yourself, collect newspaper, foam, packing tape, and boxes.

❏ Consider how you will pay any **future bills** back home. Ensure they are paid on time.

❏ Familiarize yourself with the **tax system** in your new country and lay out your finances accordingly. Consider hiring a qualified and experienced taxation adviser.

❏ Begin by **emptying** cupboards and drawers. Go through your files and folders first, then, go through your belongings and decide what you take with you and what you can leave, sell, or give away. Don't forget fixtures like lights, carpets, curtains, and kitchen appliances.

❏ Arrange for suitable temporary and/or permanent **accommodations.**

❏ Make an estimate of the **initial costs** associated with travel, shipping companies, house purchase/rental costs, furniture, car or other transportation costs, schooling, registrations, memberships, etc.

❏ Further plan your **finances** to ensure you have enough **funds** to see you through until you get settled. Keep in mind that certain things may take longer than expected, such as selling your house or searching for a new job abroad.

☐ Contact the local **social security** office to ensure that any social security/welfare benefits to which you are entitled are claimed and any for which you are no longer eligible are cancelled.

☐ If you intend to **buy property**, make an appointment with a qualified and experienced independent mortgage adviser.

☐ Obtain adequate **insurance** coverage for you and your family, including medical and dental, health, life, travel, car, household, possessions, third party liability, and holiday.

☐ Calculate enough time for the procedure to obtain your **visa** or permit.

☐ If your goal is to **work abroad,** find a suitable job or arrange for a relocation with your current employer if possible.

☐ Arrange for suitable **childcare or schooling** for your children.

☐ Prepare the following **personal documents** beforehand: Passport including passport photos, driver's license, birth certificate, marriage certificate, divorce papers, education certificates, diplomas listing any professional qualifications, language certificates, employer references, resume/C.V., medical records (including dental), banking and credit card records or salary slip showing your financial position, insurance policies, school records and reports, student records and I.D. card, and any important receipts.

❐ Make **copies and scans** of your personal documents and email them to yourself. It's annoying work but once it's done, you won't have to repeat it if you move again unless any of the documents are updated.

❐ Make all the **travel arrangements** for you and your family and plan **transport** upon arrival. If you use your own vehicle, check whether your driver's license is valid abroad.

❐ Plan a **date with the moving company** to pack and load. Ask them how long the delivery takes and if they unpack and reassemble your furniture. Make sure to keep all the items you need to carry with you aside, because movers pack up everything.

❐ **Mark** your packed boxes so you know what's in them and makes it so much easier to unpack.

Tips for learning a new language

Read through this list of tips to help you learn a new language. I have practiced all of them myself, and they are helpful for my students as well. Try them out and then make a selection to challenge yourself with every day.

☐ **Watch the local TV:**
Make an effort to watch one hour of local TV every day.

☐ **Read the Local Newspaper:**
Try reading at least 1-2 pages per day.

☐ **Venture out to local establishments:**
Get out and discover bars, shops, and local stores.

☐ **Learn a few new words everyday:**
The more words you know, the more sentences you will be able to form.

☐ **Reading:**
Whether it's a magazine or a book, even if you only look at the images and headers, you will keep picking up new vocabulary.

☐ **Etymology:**
Learning the history of the language can help you better understand it.

❏ **Immerse yourself in the language**:
Aim for a certain amount of daily exposures to the language via the methods mentioned above.

❏ **Learn the building blocks:** Teach yourself to count in the new language and learn to pronounce the letters of the alphabet.

❏ **Learn a few basic greeting words and short phrases:**
"Hello, Good morning, Goodbye, How are you? I speak English and a little (fill in the new language)."

❏ **Watch a movie in the new language**

❏ **Listen to the lyrics in your favourite music:** Find songs you like and listen to them in the local language over and over again until you start understanding some of the words.

❏ **Use Post-its:**
Write down common words and stick them everywhere in your house.

❏ **Use a language App:**

❏ **Don't be afraid to make mistakes.** Practice takes time, so be patient.

❏ **Join a language group or exchange online.** Every expat group or forum has information about languages, such as where you can find classes in your city. Also, you will easily find people to exchange languages. For example, on Internations.com, you'll find many requests such as "I want to learn Spanish and I'll teach you French in exchange". This is absolutely free of charge and a good method if you have the time and a good internet connection to meet with your language exchange partner regularly.

◻ **Get a teacher:** Receiving tailored lessons to your level and speed can be invaluable.

Money Matters

Besides planning what to see and do when you move, financial planning cannot be forgotten. Going through this list can save you from a potential financial crisis while abroad.

• **Notify your financial institutions.**
Inform your bank and credit card companies about the location of your travels and the duration of your stay in the foreign country.

• **Set up online accounts.**
With an online account, you can easily stay on top of your balances and transfers.

• **Have multiple forms of payment.**
Depending on your destination and spending habits, it's a good idea to carry a variety of payment methods such as cash, debit cards and credit cards.

- **Pay attention to safety**

Pay attention to keeping your cards, cash, and other documents safe. If you get robbed or misplace your possessions, you lose everything.

- **Emergency phone numbers**

On the back of your card you'll see an emergency phone number to cancel the card if need be. Keep these numbers written or saved somewhere together with other emergency numbers.

- **Check the exchange rates.**

Familiarize yourself with foreign currency and exchange rates to understand their value. Instead of changing money last minute at the airport or abroad, you will always find better rates on foreign currency if you plan in advance.

5. Extra fees

Be aware of extra exchange rate conversion fees when transferring money abroad.

7. Cash is king.

No one turns down cash. Carrying a couple hundred dollars or euro's worth of emergency cash is a wise decision. Remember to keep your money safe while you travel.

Accommodation

Here's a brief summary of things to consider when looking for a suitable home in your new country:

- If you are **currently a home owner,** make a decision: will you sell it, rent it, or just leave it empty?
- If you decide to **rent out your current property**, decide if you want to take care of the process yourself or employ an estate agent to manage it for you.
- Cancel your existing utility payments and contracts. When renting, remember to give proper notice. Cancel other contracts and memberships, e.g. gym membership, internet, newspaper, etc.
- Regarding your **property abroad,** make a decision about buying vs. renting and on type of accommodations you are looking for, such as an apartment or a large family home.
- **Whether you will be renting or buying**, list your requirements for your new home, e.g. number of bedrooms, parking space, garden, proximity to work, schools, shops, public transport, etc.
- Use the **internet** to research the property market in your new host country to find out what the options are including costs.
- Arrange for **temporary accommodation**, such as a hotel or rental if you cannot move in

right away upon arrival. Take into account the extra cost of this.

- If you **purchase** a property abroad, make sure you are familiar with all relevant legislation concerning property purchases by foreigners. **If renting,** decide whether you wish to move into a **fully, semi-, or non-furnished** property.

- If possible, try to **visit** the area you are considering moving to and look at it during different times of day to get a feel for the area.

- Even with extensive Google searches, a good **real estate agent** is an invaluable source of help and local information.

- When scheduling your move, if possible, make **arrangements for** the **utilities** (electricity, gas, water, internet) to be connected a day before you are due to arrive in case there are any **last-minute** problems or delays.

- Always consider the **safety and security** aspects of your new home. Thieves have a preference for expat homes.

Employment

If you intend to work abroad, here are some search ideas and job suggestions for you to consider:
- Jobs postings can be searched before moving on sites such as: LinkedIn, Indeed, Monster, Internations. Also consider consulting recruitment agencies or other expats for suggestions.
- Places to look after moving include: local schools or universities, the bulletin board (at the hostel, supermarket or library), the embassy, local online searches (LinkedIn, Monsters, Indeed, Craigslist, ...), Temporary Agencies, word of mouth in your network.

A Few Casual Job ideas:
- Language teacher
- Worker at an organic farm
- Volunteering: help prepare for Carnival in Brazil, make jewelry out of seeds in Ecuador, assist at the health centers in India, collaborate on childcare projects in Cambodia, etc.
- Au pair
- Waiter: bars, restaurants, hotels, cubs, lunch rooms, and discos
- Tourist guide or tour operator
- Cruise ship worker
- Entertainer: organizing activities for guests at holiday resorts or hotels.
- Diving instructor

Tasks to do upon arrival (if not done in advance)

- ☐ Register with your local embassy or consulate (if possible)
- ☐ Register with the local municipality (mandatory)
- ☐ Collect or arrange a residence permit and/or work permit
- ☐ Arrange for a local bank account
- ☐ Arrange for local health insurance (mandatory)
- ☐ Obtain a driver's license or exchange your current license
- ☐ Get connected: arrange for internet, phone, and utilities (gas, electricity, water, TV)
- ☐ Register with a local doctor and dentist
- ☐ Find or move into your new accommodations
- ☐ Investigate school/childcare options
- ☐ Consider introducing yourself to your neighbours
- ☐ Make sure you keep the ones back home informed during your move abroad
- ☐ A mobile phone is essential to communicate. You may use your own service provider temporarily, but beware of hefty usage fees. You will want to switch to a local provider soon after you arrive. Remember to notify friends and family of your new number.
- ☐ Internet at home may take a while; rely on public Wi-Fi, restaurants, the library, or internet cafés to get online. Depending where you are, the connection may be difficult, slow or bad, but that's part of amusing expat journey.

Settle in Smoothly

☐ **Things you can do with other people:**

    ☐ Develop a support network in your new country

    ☐ Invite people over to your house (e.g. neighbours, colleague)

    ☐ Visit someone else (colleague, neighbour)

    ☐ Call or skype with your family and friends

    ☐ Go to a movie, cafe, etc. and enjoy the entertainment options

    ☐ Join online expat chat groups

    ☐ Participate in a team sport or fitness class

    ☐ Work as a volunteer for a good cause

    ☐ Join a choir.

    ☐ Join a gym or any other exercise group.

    ☐ Find a cycle, walking, or running group

    ☐ Join meetup groups, club or association

    ☐ Get active in the local and/or expat community

    ☐ Go to a church or other local faith community.

    ☐ Make friends with the locals who can provide you information that other expats can't give you.

☐ **Things you can do on your own:**

    ☐ Read books, newspaper, magazines, internet

    ☐ Listen to music

    ☐ Cook a meal

- ❏ Take a walk outside
- ❏ Meditate
- ❏ Go to the movie theater
- ❏ Write in your journal
- ❏ Go to a restaurant or cafe
- ❏ Go shopping
- ❏ Watch your favourite movie
- ❏ Exercise outside or at the gym
- ❏ Take pictures
- ❏ Become a member of the library and find local events advertised there
- ❏ Check tourist information offices for local events.
- ❏ Play an instrument
- ❏ Take a ride by bike, car, or bus
- ❏ Practice a craft
- ❏ Go to the local market
- ❏ Simply sit and watch.
- ❏ Take a trip
- ❏ Watch television
- ❏ Watch people while sitting at different places
- ❏ Study a new language (check out the checklist on languages!)

❏ Thoughts to remember during difficult moments
- ❏ This too will pass.
- ❏ It's not the end of the world.
- ❏ I came here to experience a challenge.
- ❏ I've been through worse than this.

179

- ❏ It's natural to feel down from time to time, no matter where I am.
- ❏ No pain; no gain.
- ❏ It's not just me.
- ❏ Things didn't always go well back home either.
- ❏ I have taken on a lot; I should expect to feel overwhelmed from time to time.
- ❏ I have already accomplished a lot in my time here; I can do this!

You've reached THE END of this book.

The beginning of your journey is waiting for YOU.

Bibliography

Chaney, L., Martin, J. (2014). *Intercultural Business Communication.* Essex, UK: Pearson.

Hall, E.T., (1976). Beyond Culture. Garden City, NY: Doubleday Anchor Books.

Hofstede, G., Hofstede, G-J., Minkov, M. (2010) *Cultures and Organizations: Software of the Mind.* London, UK: McGraw-Hill.

Lustig, M.W., Koester, J., Halualani, R. (2017). *Intercultural Competence: Interpersonal*

Communication Across Cultures. New York, NY: Pearson.

Morris, J., Pahladsingh, S. (2017). *The Eight Great Beacons of Cultural Awareness.* Zaltbommel, The Netherlands: Thema.

Nunez,C., Nunez, R.M., Popma, L. (2014). *Intercultural sensitivity: From Denial to Intercultural Competence.* Assen, The Netherlands: Royal Van Gorcum.

Trompenaars, F. (2012).*Riding the Waves of Culture: Understanding Diversity in Global*

Business. London, UK: Nicholas Brealey Publishing.

Did you enjoy this book?

Thank you so much for reading **Living Abroad Successfully: What, Where, When, How.** I hope you enjoyed reading this book even half as much as I enjoyed creating it for you.

A repeat read is highly recommended. Each time you pick it up again, you will learn and discover new things.

If you enjoyed this book, please leave a review. It really helps and I would be so grateful!

May I also recommend being a good friend by sharing this book with someone in your life who could benefit from the material.

This book you hold in your hands is meant to cover the basics with regards to moving abroad. There is much more I had wanted to include but couldn't due to space constraints. This book is a guideline, a blueprint to get you moving. Additional information may be necessary along the way, depending on your personal situation. However, with this book you have the basics you need to begin your journey!

For more suggestions, reading materials, and videos on improving your confidence, adjusting to a new culture, or living as an expat, please find me online.

Website: http://www.rachelsmets.com
Facebook: https://www.facebook.com/1.RachelSmets/
YouTube: http://bit.ly/YouTube-RachelSmets
TED^x http://bit.ly/RachelSmets-TEDxTalk
Book: *Awaken Your Confidence: 15 People Share Their Journey to Success.* Available on Amazon:
http://bit.ly/AwakenYourConfidence

If you didn't get your **FREE GIFT** at the beginning of my book, you can still get it here: http://www.rachelsmets.com/living-abroad-successfully-free-gift

If you have any questions, comments, or feedback, please don't hesitate to contact me. I'd love to hear from you.

Thanks again for reading, and best of luck!

Rachel

http://amzn.to/2cl425Q

ABOUT THE AUTHOR

Rachel is a speaker, lecturer, trainer, and bestselling author.

Living and working in several countries for many years, she developed a passion for cultures and languages. Besides boosting people's confidence through coaching, she enjoys providing inter-cultural business training and teaching conversational languages, both online and offline.

Rachel motivates and inspires people by sharing her own journey in her straightforward and down-to-earth style.

She graduated from the University of Maryland (US) with a bachelor's degree in psychology, and achieved her master's degree in management from the University of St. Andrews (UK).

Born and raised in Belgium, Rachel started her expat life in 2003. Learning about other people and experiencing different cultures is her passion, and she is thrilled to be living the life she has chosen for herself and deeply enjoys helping others by sharing her experiences.

Striving, sure, social and sportive, she keeps her mind & body in balance by exercising daily, either running outside or lifting weights at the gym.

Rachel enjoys motivating and inspiring people to become the person they want to be.
Life changes, and so can you!

You can find out more on her website:
http://www.rachelsmets.com

Check out her latest online course on Udemy:
Tools to overcome fear and take control.
http://bit.ly/UdemyTakeControl

For more updates and videos, please go to her You Tube or Facebook.

Find her book on Amazon, *Awaken Your Confidence: 15 People Share their Journey to Success*

Made in United States
Orlando, FL
14 November 2023

38957760R00102